The Future of Care "A Digital Roadmap for Healthcare Systems"

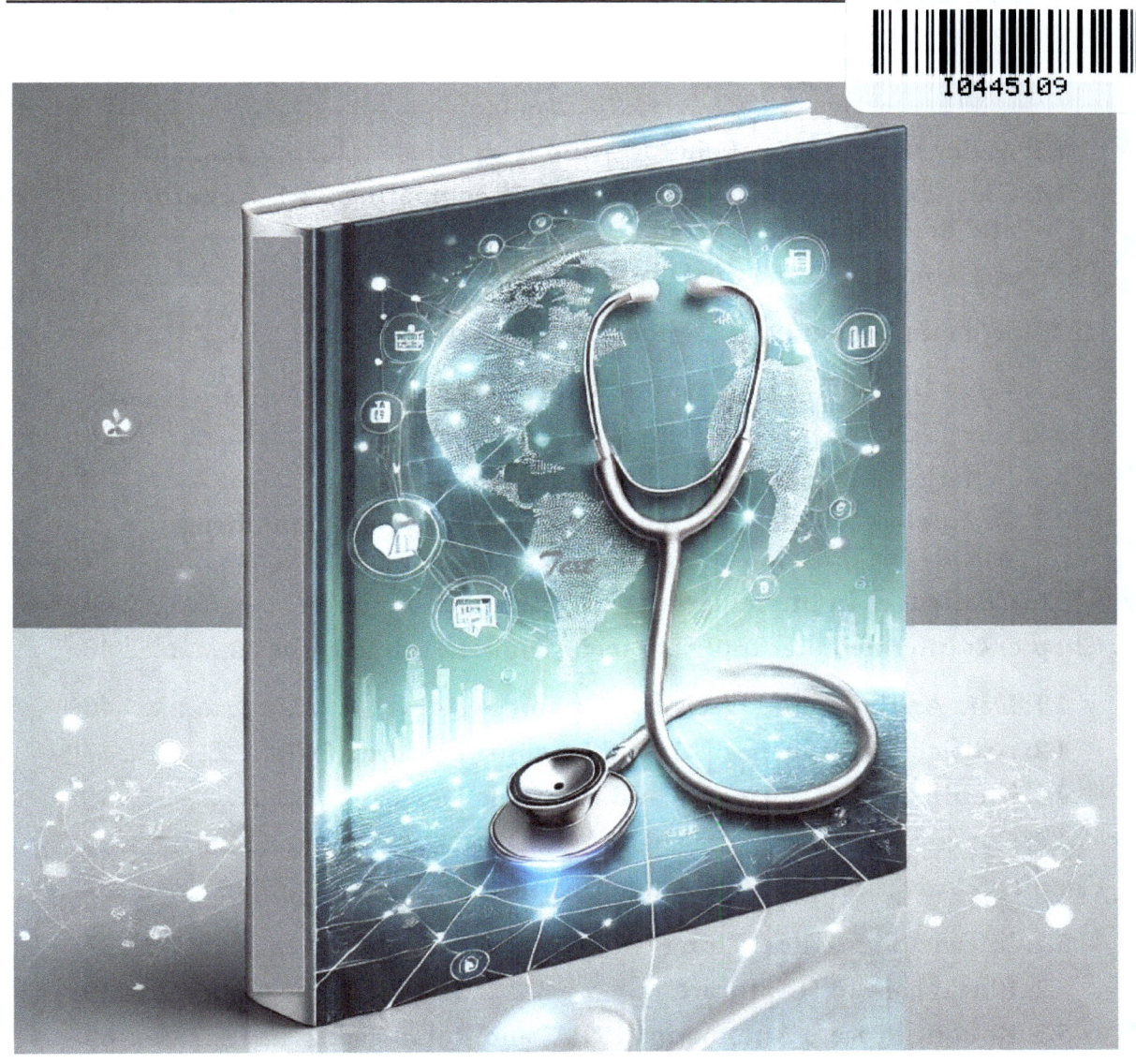

Table of Contents

Dedication 4

Preface 5

About the Author 6

Chapter 1: Introduction to Healthcare Digital Transformation 7
    1.1: Overview of the Healthcare Industry 7
    1.2: Healthcare System Models 9
    1.3: Major healthcare stakeholders and their roles 10
    1.4: Global variations in healthcare models: comparing the U.S., Europe, and developing nations 11

Chapter 2: Understanding the Healthcare Business Model 16

Chapter 3: Fundamentals of Digital Transformation 20
    3.1: What Digital Transformation Really Means 20
    3.2: Key Technologies in Digital Transformation 21
    3.4: Benefits of Digital Transformation in Healthcare 38
    3.5: Technology vendors, system integrators, and consulting firms worldwide 39
    3.6: Challenges in Implementing Digital Transformation 44

Chapter 4: Intermediate Applications of Digital Technologies 46
    4.1: Data Analytics and Decision Support Systems 46
    4.2: Artificial Intelligence (AI) and Machine Learning (ML) 47
    4.3: Mobile Health (mHealth) and Wearable Devices 55
    4.4: Cybersecurity in Healthcare 56

Chapter 5: Advanced Digital Transformation Solutions 57
    5.1: Internet of Medical Things (IoMT) 57
    5.2: Blockchain in Healthcare 59
    5.3: Robotic Process Automation (RPA) and Robotics 60

Chapter 6: Strategic Implementation of Digital Transformation in Healthcare 62

    6.1: Building a Digital Transformation Strategy 62

    6.2: Leadership and Change Management 64

Chapter 7: Emerging Trends and the Future of Healthcare Digital Transformation 66

    7.1: Precision Medicine and Genomics 66

    7.2: Virtual Reality (VR) and Augmented Reality (AR) in healthcare ... 67

    7.3: 3D Printing and Bioprinting 68

Chapter 8: The Quintuple Aim Framework and Its Role in Digital Transformation 69

    Introduction 69

    The Quintuple Aim and Digital Transformation Goals 70

Chapter 9: Aligning the Target Operating Model (TOM) with Healthcare's Digital Transformation Goals 72

Chapter 10: The Vision for a Unified Medical Database and Advanced Care Management System 79

Chapter 11: Understanding HL7 and FHIR in Healthcare

Chapter 12: ConsultCare: A Catalyst for Digital Healthcare Transformation 91

Chapter 13: A Holistic Digital Transformation Roadmap 98

    Introduction: Building the Future of Healthcare Together 98

    7-Step Roadmap to Healthcare Transformation 98

Chapter 14: Global Digital Transformation in Healthcare: Innovations Across Regions 103

A Shared Mission for the Future of Care 107

Appendix A: Cross-Reference of the Quintuple Aim with Key Book Chapters 108

Appendix B: Healthcare Digital Transformation Taxonomy 110

Appendix C: List of Abbreviations 115

Dedication

This book is dedicated to my mother (Aida), whose strength, resilience, and unwavering trust in God during her emergency situation and stay in the ICU (Intensive Care Unit) for two weeks outside of her country inspired this effort. Last year, my mother faced a life-threatening situation in the emergency care unit. She was on the verge of undergoing heart surgery an unnecessary and potentially dangerous procedure — simply because her doctors did not have access to the most up-to-date information about her medical history, lab results, and diagnostic reports.

The incident was a turning point for me. It revealed how the lack of real-time, accurate medical data can lead to serious errors in care and patients' sufferings. I realized that the future of healthcare must include systems that connect patients' information seamlessly, empowering healthcare providers to make informed decisions in real-time and preventing such near-misses. My mother's experience brought to light the urgent need for innovation in healthcare systems that are not only efficient but also safe, patient-centered, and capable of delivering the right care at the right time.

I hope that this work serves as a step towards a future where no one else has to face the uncertainty my mother experienced, and where every patient can trust that their care will be based on the most accurate and timely information available.

To my lovely mother, thank you for inspiring me to act. This book is for you, and for every patient whose safety and well-being depend on a connected and informed healthcare system.

Preface

The Future of Care: A Digital Roadmap for Healthcare Systems is a guide to the profound transformation happening in the healthcare sector, driven by technology. This book was born from a deep personal experience that shaped my understanding of the challenges and opportunities within healthcare today. Several years ago, my mother was almost subjected to an unnecessary heart surgery due to the lack of real-time access to her medical records, lab results, and diagnostic imaging. This experience highlighted a critical gap in healthcare disconnected systems that fail to deliver timely and accurate information when it's most needed.

This book aims to address that gap by exploring how digital technologies can revolutionize healthcare systems. It outlines a roadmap to create a future where healthcare is smarter, more connected, and safer for all patients. I focus on how technologies like Artificial Intelligence (AI), the Internet of Medical Things (IoMT), and blockchain can empower healthcare providers and improve the quality of care, operational efficiency, and patient outcomes.

The chapters in this book offer both strategic frameworks and practical steps for embracing the digital future of healthcare. From building a unified medical database to leveraging advanced AI-powered solutions, each chapter serves as a guide for healthcare leaders, policymakers, and technologists who are ready to innovate and move toward a more integrated, patient-centered healthcare system.

About the Author

Diaa ElDin Helmy is a digital transformation strategist with over two decades of experience helping organizations unlock their potential through innovative technology. Currently serving as the Sales Director for Consulting and Professional Services at Oracle Saudi Arabia, Diaa specializes in turning complex challenges into impactful solutions, particularly in healthcare, and public services.

Diaa's career is rooted in a passion for enabling organizations to deliver better outcomes through technology. With expertise in areas like artificial intelligence, cloud solutions, and enterprise resource planning (ERP), he has led teams to achieve record-breaking growth and helped clients modernize their operations to align with cutting-edge technologies.

A lifelong learner, Diaa holds an MBA in International Management and certifications in AI and healthcare technology. He is a strong advocate for collaboration and innovation, and his work reflects a commitment to improving the lives of patients and empowering healthcare providers with the tools they need to succeed.

Chapter 1: Introduction to Healthcare Digital Transformation

1.1: Overview of the Healthcare Industry

In this chapter, you will explore the basic structure of healthcare systems, from public to private models, and how they operate globally. You'll gain insight into the key stakeholders like patients, providers, regulators, and payers. The chapter will also discuss pressing issues like cost containment, accessibility, and healthcare inequality.

What is Healthcare?

Imagine a world without hospitals, doctors, or even medicine. Healthcare is something we often take for granted, but it plays a vital role in our lives by helping us stay healthy, recover when we're sick, and, ideally, live longer, healthier lives. The healthcare industry exists to meet these needs on a large scale, covering everything from routine check-ups to complex surgeries, vaccinations to mental health support.

Here's a quick look at the major areas of healthcare:

- **Preventative Care**: Services like immunizations, health screenings, and education aim to stop diseases before they start.
- **Curative Care**: This involves diagnosing and treating illnesses, whether through medication, surgery, or other methods.

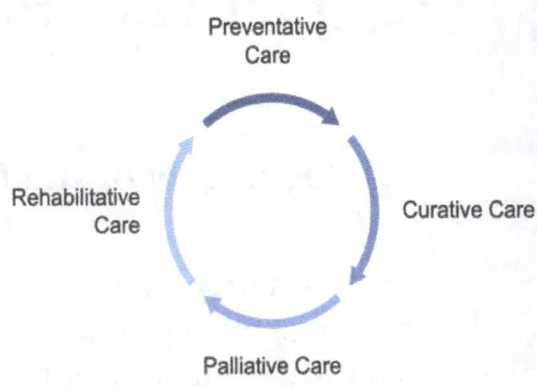

- **Palliative Care**: When a person is dealing with a serious, life-limiting illness, palliative care focuses on providing comfort rather than a cure.
- **Rehabilitative Care**: This is all about recovery, helping patients regain abilities after events like strokes or surgeries.

Each area has unique goals and approaches, but together, they create a safety net for our health.

1.2: Healthcare System Models

Healthcare is delivered differently worldwide. Here are the four main models:

1. **Beveridge Model**: Funded and managed by the government, like the U.K.'s NHS. Think of it as healthcare funded by taxes, provided to everyone, free at the point of use.

2. **Bismarck Model**: Found in countries like Germany, where employers and employees pay for healthcare through insurance, and hospitals are often private.

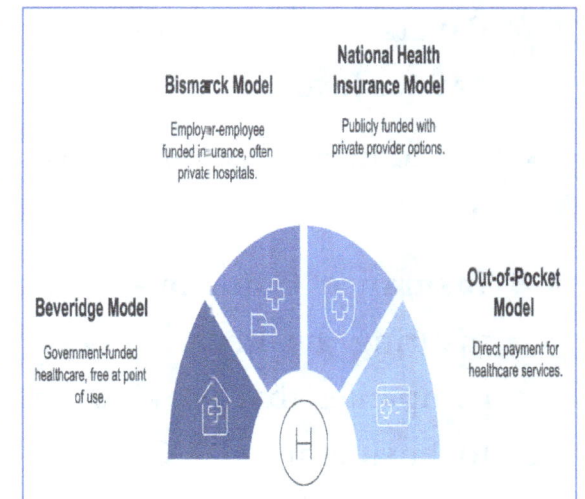

3. **National Health Insurance Model**: A combination of the Beveridge and Bismarck models, as seen in Canada. It's publicly funded but allows private providers.

4. **Out-of-Pocket Model**: In some places, if you need healthcare, you simply pay out-of-pocket. This is more common in countries with limited healthcare infrastructure or support.

1.3: Major healthcare stakeholders and their roles

The healthcare world revolves around several main players:

- **Patients**: That's all of us at some point! Patients are the focus, with a goal of improving health and quality of life.

- **Providers**: These are the doctors, nurses, and hospitals delivering care.

- **Payers**: Insurance companies, governments, or individuals who pay for healthcare services.

- **Regulators**: Organizations that oversee and ensure healthcare quality and safety, like the FDA in the U.S. or WHO globally.

- **Insurance Companies:** These are either the public funds for insuring healthcare beneficiaries, or the private commercial companies that provides insurance policies either B2B (business to business) or B2C (Business to consumer). After applying a policy validations and payment premiums.

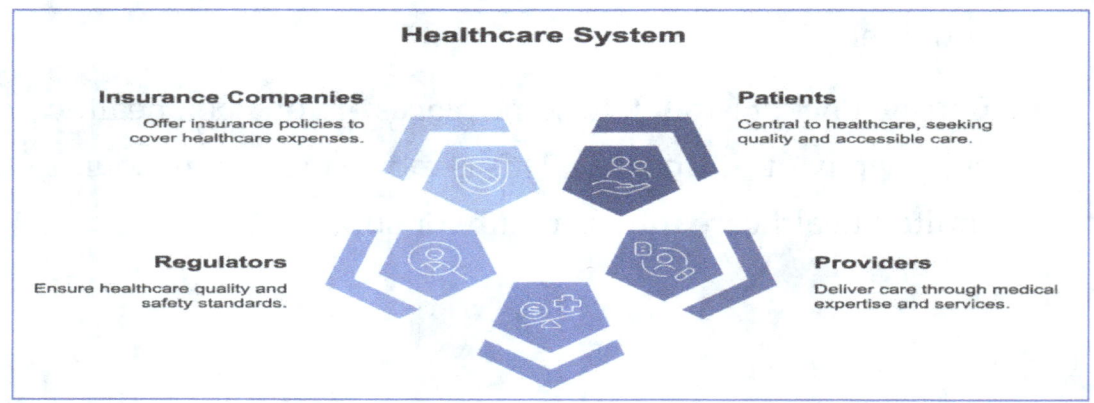

Each group has different priorities, and sometimes they clash. For example, patients want quality and accessibility, but payers might focus on managing costs. This push-and-pull creates complexity in healthcare systems.

1.4: Global variations in healthcare models: comparing the U.S., Europe, and developing nations

Healthcare models vary significantly around the world due to differences in funding, accessibility, and healthcare delivery methods. Let's compare the U.S., European countries, and developing nations, highlighting key distinctions.

The United States: Market-Based and Mixed System

The U.S. healthcare system is a unique combination of private and public funding, with a largely market-driven approach:

- **Private Insurance Dominance**: Most Americans receive health insurance through private, employer-based plans, with individuals often required to pay premiums, co-pays, and deductibles.
- **Public Programs for Vulnerable Groups**: Government-funded programs like Medicare (for elderly individuals), Medicaid (for low-income individuals), and the Veterans Health Administration (for military veterans) offer coverage but are limited to specific populations.
- **High Costs and Innovation**: The U.S. spends more per capita on healthcare than any other country, largely due to high administrative costs, advanced medical technologies, and

pharmaceutical pricing. While this leads to high-quality healthcare for those with access, it also results in significant disparities.

- **Challenges with Accessibility**: Unlike many other developed countries, the U.S. does not offer universal healthcare. People without insurance, especially low-income individuals, face barriers to accessing care, despite reforms like the Affordable Care Act (ACA) that aimed to expand coverage.

Europe: Publicly Funded and Universal Coverage Models

Many European countries follow universal coverage models, focusing on accessibility and affordability for all citizens. However, there are variations across the region:

- **Beveridge Model (e.g., U.K., Spain)**: In the U.K. and Spain, healthcare is primarily funded and provided by the government. Services are free at the point of care, and funding comes through general taxation. The National Health Service (NHS) in the U.K. is a classic example of this model.

- **Bismarck Model (e.g., Germany, France)**: Germany and France use a system of social health insurance funded by employers and employees through payroll deductions. Care is provided by both public and private institutions, and insurance is mandatory, with subsidies for low-income citizens.

- **Single-Payer Hybrid Models (e.g., Scandinavian countries)**: In countries like Sweden and Denmark, healthcare is taxpayer-funded and provided mainly by government institutions, but there is also some private-sector involvement, particularly in specialized services.

European models prioritize **equity and accessibility**, making healthcare affordable for all citizens and residents. Waiting times for certain services can be longer, but overall satisfaction levels are high, and health outcomes are generally favorable.

Developing Nations: Out-of-Pocket and Limited Access Models

In many developing countries, healthcare systems face significant challenges due to limited resources, infrastructure, and funding:

- **Out-of-Pocket Payments**: A large portion of healthcare expenses in developing countries is paid out-of-pocket by individuals. This approach leads to financial burdens for those with limited income, often forcing families into poverty due to medical costs.

- **Public Systems with Resource Constraints**: Some developing nations, like India and Nigeria, have public health systems, but these often lack the funding, personnel, and facilities needed to serve the entire population effectively. Access to care in rural areas can be especially limited.

- **International Aid and Non-Governmental Support**: Organizations like the World Health Organization (WHO), World Bank, and various NGOs play a significant role in supporting healthcare in developing countries, particularly in areas like vaccinations, maternal health, and disease control (e.g., HIV, malaria).

- **Fragmented Services and Health Inequities**: Healthcare in developing nations is often unevenly distributed, with urban centers receiving better resources than rural areas. Health inequities persist due to income disparities, infrastructure gaps, and limited education on health practices.

Key Comparative Takeaways

- **Access to Healthcare**: European countries and some developing nations aim for universal access, though resources and infrastructure limitations in developing countries hinder effectiveness. The U.S. system, while advanced, struggles with accessibility for uninsured populations.

- **Funding and Affordability**: European systems focus on taxpayer-funded or employer-supported insurance, making healthcare affordable. In contrast, the U.S. relies heavily on private insurance with significant out-of-pocket costs, while developing nations often lack adequate funding.

- **Quality and Efficiency**: The U.S. leads in technology and innovation, often delivering high-quality care for those who can afford it. Europe balances quality with accessibility through its universal models, while developing countries face challenges in maintaining quality due to resource constraints.

Each model reflects a trade-off among quality, accessibility, and cost, shaped by the unique economic, political, and social contexts of each region.

Challenges in delivering consistent care: disparities, access, and infrastructure

Healthcare around the world faces big challenges, but there are also exciting trends:

- **Aging Populations**: People are living longer, which means healthcare systems must handle more age-related conditions like arthritis or dementia.

- **Chronic Illness**: Issues like heart disease, diabetes, and asthma require ongoing care, putting a lot of strain on healthcare systems.

- **Rising Costs and Access Issues**: As healthcare advances, it often becomes more expensive. Many people still lack access to basic services, and high costs can make it difficult for some to get the care they need.

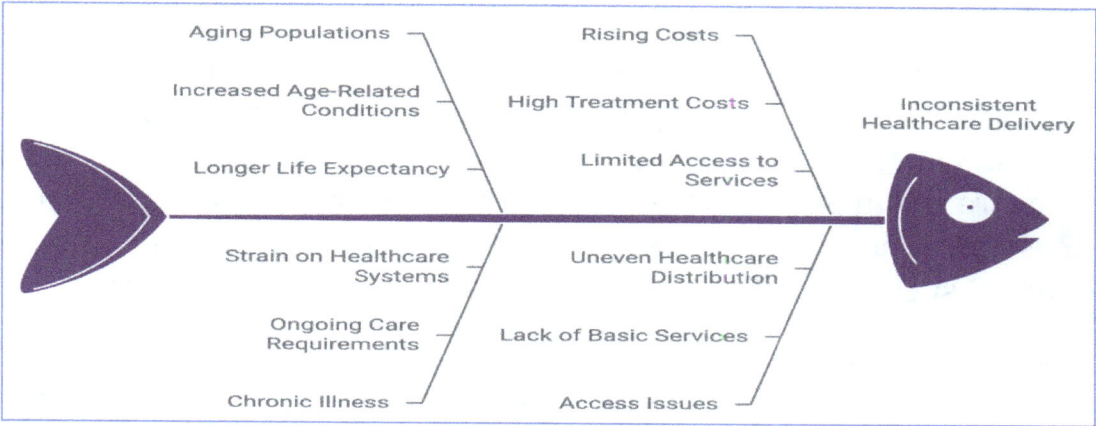

There are also trends shaping healthcare's future:

- **Closing Health Gaps**: Digital health tools are helping improve access and quality of care, especially in underserved areas.

- **Personalized Medicine**: Tailoring treatment to an individual's genetic profile is becoming possible thanks to new technology.

- Unified universal Real-time care management and clinical system.

Chapter 2: Understanding the Healthcare Business Model

Introduction

Healthcare organizations operate within a highly dynamic and complex ecosystem, where balancing patient outcomes, operational efficiency, and financial sustainability is critical. A clear understanding of the healthcare business model reveals how organizations attract patients, deliver care, and manage resources while adapting to evolving industry demands, such as digital transformation and value-based care.

This chapter explores the healthcare business model, providing insights into its strategic pillars, core processes, and emerging trends shaping the industry's future.

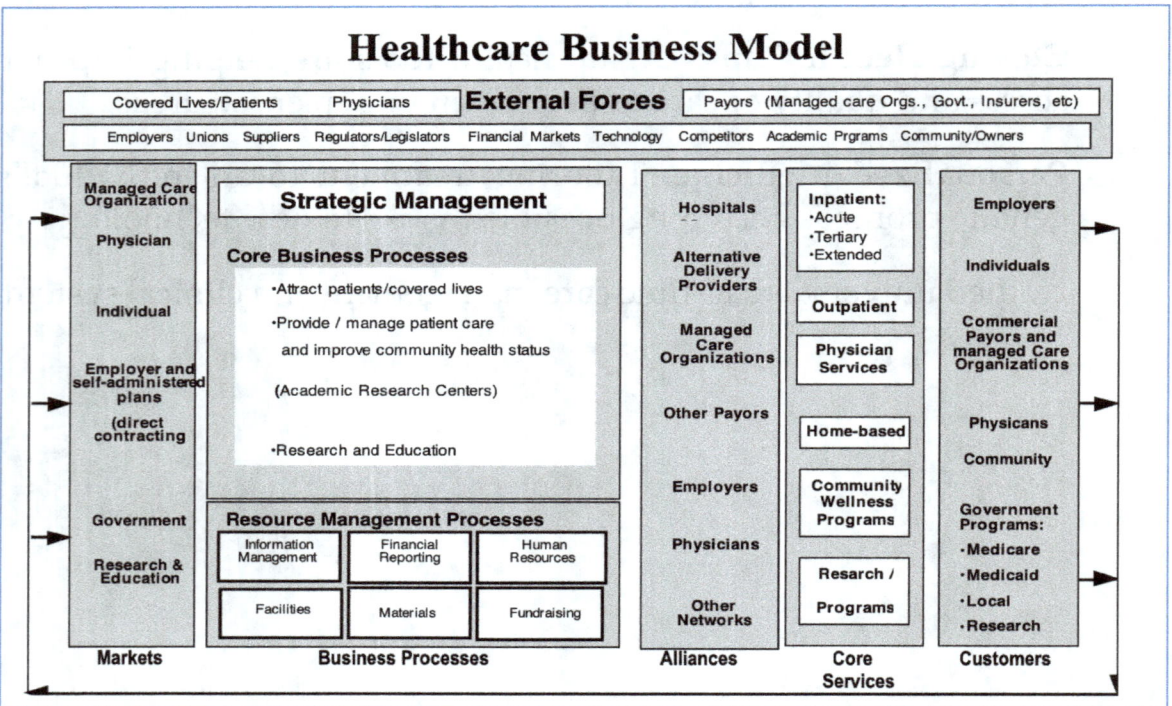

Pillars of the Healthcare Business Model

The healthcare business model is structured around three fundamental pillars:

1. **Strategic Management**:

    - Establishing long-term objectives to improve patient care, community health, and organizational efficiency.

    - Aligning operations with external influences, including government regulations, patient demographics, and competitive pressures.

    - Value-Based Care: Transitioning from traditional fee-for-service models to value-based approaches that reward improved patient outcomes.

    - Population Health Strategies: Addressing social determinants of health and implementing community-based interventions.

    - Care Innovation: Leveraging technologies like AI, IoT, and blockchain to enhance patient safety, reduce errors, and optimize care delivery.

2. **Core Processes**:

    - Attracting Patients: Through public outreach, partnerships with payers, and leveraging digital tools for enhanced accessibility.

    - Launching health education campaigns to encourage early screenings.

    - Expanding telehealth services to improve access for rural communities.

- Building strong networks with insurance companies and referral organizations.
- **Delivering Care:** Managing the patient journey from preventive care to specialized treatments and post-care coordination.
- Streamlining workflows with integrated electronic health records (EHRs).
- Enhancing patient engagement through mobile health apps and personalized care plans.
- Reducing clinical errors by adopting AI-powered decision support systems.

3. **Resource Management:**
   - **Financial Resources:** Implementing cost-control measures, improving revenue cycle management, and aligning reimbursement models with care delivery outcomes.
   - **Human Resources:** Addressing staffing shortages, providing ongoing training for digital technologies, and enhancing employee satisfaction to reduce burnout.
   - **Technology and Facilities:** Investing in modern infrastructure, such as IoT devices for patient monitoring and digital twins for operational optimization.

Trends Shaping the Future of Healthcare Business Models

The healthcare industry is rapidly transforming due to emerging trends:

- **Digital Transformation**: Technologies like FHIR-based interoperability, cloud platforms, and wearable devices enable seamless data sharing and real-time care delivery.

- **Patient-Centered Care**: Increasing focus on patient empowerment, such as allowing patients access to their health data through apps like MyChart or Apple Health.

- **Telehealth and Remote Care**: Expanding telemedicine solutions to address care gaps while reducing costs and improving convenience for patients.

- **Sustainability**: Implementing environmentally friendly practices, such as energy-efficient facilities and green supply chains.

Challenges and Opportunities

Healthcare organizations face several challenges, including:

- Navigating stringent regulatory environments.
- Rising operational costs due to advanced technology adoption.
- Adapting to shifting patient expectations for personalized, technology-driven care.

However, significant opportunities exist in adopting value-based care models, leveraging AI for predictive analytics, and embracing partnerships with technology firms to co-develop innovative solutions.

Chapter 3: Fundamentals of Digital Transformation

This chapter introduces the foundational concepts and benefits of digital transformation in healthcare. By using relatable language and real-world examples, it helps readers understand why digital transformation is essential and what it entails.

3.1: What Digital Transformation Really Means

Digital transformation can sound like a buzzword, but at its core, it's about using digital technology to make processes, systems, and people work better together. Think of it as "modernizing" with a purpose: not just adding tech for the sake of it but finding ways that technology can truly improve the way things are done.

In healthcare, this could mean anything from switching from paper records to digital ones to using artificial intelligence (AI) to help diagnose diseases faster.

Why Healthcare Needs Digital Transformation

Imagine walking into a hospital where:

- Doctors already have your full medical history, accessible in seconds.
- You can schedule a virtual check-up without leaving home.
- Emergency teams use real-time data to prepare before you even arrive.
- You can have access to a unified updated healthcare file for you and your family members at any time.

Digital transformation is making these scenarios a reality. By helping healthcare systems operate more efficiently, it aims to reduce costs, improve patient outcomes, and create a smoother experience for patients and healthcare providers alike.

3.2: Key Technologies in Digital Transformation

1. **Electronic Health Records (EHRs) Vs. Electronic Medical Record (EMRs)**

The key difference between **Electronic Medical Records (EMRs)** and **Electronic Health Records (EHRs)** lies in their scope and purpose.

EMR (Electronic Medical Record):

> **Definition**: An EMR is a digital version of a patient's paper chart, containing medical and treatment history from a single healthcare provider or facility.
>
> **Scope**: It is limited to a specific practice or organization. It holds medical data like diagnoses, treatments, and medications for internal use by healthcare providers.
>
> **Usage**: Primarily for tracking a patient's health within a single provider's office. It's used for diagnosing and treating patients, but its data is not easily shared outside the facility.

EHR (Electronic Health Record):

Definition: An EHR is a more comprehensive digital record that includes all of the patient's health information, from multiple healthcare providers.

Scope: EHRs are designed to share information across different healthcare organizations, including specialists, laboratories, hospitals, and clinics.

Usage: EHRs support a broader view of patient care. They allow for easier data sharing between various healthcare providers, ensuring continuity of care. They include more detailed and longitudinal information such as medical histories, test results, allergies, and comprehensive treatment plans.

HIS (Health Information System)

Definition: A broad, integrated system used to manage healthcare data across an organization. It encompasses not just patient medical records, but also administrative, financial, and operational data. HIS integrates various subsystems to improve the efficiency and quality of care, while also managing resources, staff, and finances within healthcare settings.

Scope: HIS spans the entire healthcare organization or network. It integrates various systems for managing clinical data (EHR/EMR), financial data (billing, insurance), administrative data (patient scheduling), and other operational tasks (staff management, inventory, etc.). HIS enables the seamless flow of information across different departments and stakeholders within the healthcare facility.

Usage: HISs Supports healthcare management, improves clinical care, enhances operational efficiency, and aids decision-making.

Here's a table summarizing the differences between EMR, HER and HIS:

Feature	EMR (Electronic Medical Record)	EHR (Electronic Health Record)	HIS (Health Information System)
Definition	A digital version of a patient's medical chart, typically used within one healthcare provider or facility.	A more comprehensive digital record of a patient's health information, used across multiple healthcare providers.	A broader system that integrates and manages various types of healthcare data, such as clinical, administrative, and financial data.
Scope	Limited to a single healthcare provider or facility.	Designed to be shared across different healthcare organizations and systems.	Encompasses the entire healthcare organization or network, including clinical, financial, and operational data.

Feature	EMR (Electronic Medical Record)	EHR (Electronic Health Record)	HIS (Health Information System)
Purpose	Primarily for tracking patient care within a specific provider's office or clinic.	To provide a complete, longitudinal view of a patient's health history, supporting continuity of care across providers.	To manage all aspects of a healthcare organization's operations, including patient data, financial records, staff management, and more.
Interoperability	Limited; primarily used within one facility or practice.	High; facilitates sharing patient data across multiple providers, enhancing care coordination.	High; connects and integrates multiple systems within a healthcare organization for seamless data flow.

Feature	EMR (Electronic Medical Record)	EHR (Electronic Health Record)	HIS (Health Information System)
Data Included	Patient's medical history, diagnoses, treatment plans, medications, lab results (within one provider).	A full spectrum of a patient's health information, including medical history, medications, lab results, imaging, allergies, and treatment history from multiple sources.	Includes patient data (EHR/EMR), administrative data (scheduling, billing), and financial information (accounts payable/receivable, insurance).
Users	Primarily used by healthcare providers (e.g., doctors, nurses) within a single facility.	Used by various healthcare providers, specialists, and facilities involved in the patient's care.	Used by administrators, clinicians, staff, and managers within a healthcare organization.

Feature	EMR (Electronic Medical Record)	EHR (Electronic Health Record)	HIS (Health Information System)
Example	A doctor's office using an EMR system to store patient visits and treatment notes.	A hospital network sharing a patient's health records across multiple departments and providers.	A hospital's complete management system that integrates patient records (EHR), scheduling, billing, and payroll.

Key Takeaways from Current EHR Systems and the Need for Innovation

This document outlines the limitations of current Electronic Health Record (EHR) systems and emphasizes the necessity for a new approach to enhance clinician workflow and patient care. It also highlights Oracle's vision for a connected healthcare ecosystem through innovative EHR solutions that prioritize clinician needs.

Limitations of Current EHR Systems.

- **Designed for Revenue Cycle Management:** Current EHR systems were primarily developed with a focus on revenue cycle management rather than optimizing clinician workflow. This misalignment often leads to inefficiencies in patient care.

- **Closed Systems:** Many EHRs operate as closed systems, which restricts data sharing and interoperability. This lack of integration can hinder comprehensive patient care and limit the ability to share critical information across different healthcare providers.

- **Contributing to Clinician Burnout:** The administrative burdens associated with EHRs can lead to increased clinician burnout. The time spent on documentation and navigating complex systems detracts from the time available for patient interaction and care.

The Need for a New Approach

To address the challenges faced by healthcare today, a new generation of EHRs is essential. The focus of these systems should be on:

- Improving Clinician Experience: EHRs must be designed with the clinician's workflow in mind, making it easier for them to access and input information without unnecessary complications.

- Reducing Administrative Tasks: Streamlining administrative processes will allow clinicians to spend more time on patient care rather than paperwork.

- Facilitating Data Sharing: A more open and interoperable system is needed to ensure that healthcare providers can easily share and access patient data, leading to better-informed clinical decisions.

  In conclusion, the evolution of EHR systems is crucial for improving healthcare delivery. By focusing on clinician needs and fostering a connected ecosystem, healthcare technology organizations should collaborate to pave the way for a more efficient and effective healthcare system.

2. Telemedicine

- **What It Is**: Healthcare services provided remotely through video calls, phone, or apps.
- **Why It's Transformative**: Telemedicine expands access to care, especially for people in rural areas or those unable to travel. During

the COVID-19 pandemic, telemedicine became essential, proving its value for the future.

3. Artificial Intelligence (AI) and Machine Learning (ML)

- **What They Are**: AI refers to computers simulating human intelligence, and ML is a subset that allows computers to learn from data.
- **Applications in Healthcare**: AI and ML are used for early disease detection, predicting patient outcomes, and automating administrative tasks. For instance, AI tools can review medical images faster and with a high degree of accuracy, helping radiologists detect issues like cancer in its early stages.

4. Wearable Devices and IoT (Internet of Things)

- **What They Are**: Smartwatches, fitness trackers, and medical devices that collect real-time health data, often connected via the Internet of Things.
- **Why They're Important**: Wearables track health metrics like heart rate, sleep patterns, and activity levels. This data can help doctors monitor chronic conditions remotely and provide patients with a personalized healthcare experience.

5. ERP Solutions for Healthcare

- **What They Are**: Imagine a hospital as a busy orchestra, with each department playing its part to provide patient care. Sometimes, though, the "music" can feel a bit chaotic departments don't communicate well, supplies run out, or billing becomes a headache.

This is where **Enterprise Resource Planning (ERP) solutions come in.**

An ERP system is like the conductor of the orchestra. It brings together all the moving parts—finance, human resources, supply chain, and patient administration—onto one platform. Instead of each department working in isolation, an ERP system connects them so they can share information and operate as a harmonious whole.

- **Why they are important:** ERP provides real-time data that helps hospital leaders make informed choices, Automation cuts down on repetitive tasks, leaving staff free to focus on patients, faster appointments to clearer bills, ERP makes the experience smoother for everyone, As hospitals expand, ERP systems grow with them, making it easier to add new departments or services.

ERP Automation vs Digital Transformation in Healthcare

Element	Automation (ERP in Healthcare)	Digital Transformation (ERP in Healthcare)
Definition	Use of ERP systems to automate routine administrative and clinical tasks such as scheduling, billing, and inventory management.	ERP systems are integrated into healthcare digital transformation to enhance patient care, data sharing, and decision-making.
Scope	Focuses on improving efficiency in specific areas like patient billing, inventory, HR, and supply chain management without changing care models.	Involves rethinking entire healthcare delivery models by integrating ERP with digital health tools, telemedicine, and data analytics.
Goals	Streamline administrative workflows, reduce manual errors, and improve resource management within healthcare facilities.	Utilize ERP as a core component to enable patient-centric care, enhance clinical outcomes, and improve operational agility.

Outcomes	Increases administrative efficiency, reduces paperwork, and ensures compliance with regulations through automated reporting.	Enhances patient experience through better data availability, faster diagnostics, personalized treatments, and improved care coordination.
Focus	Automates repetitive and administrative tasks in ERP systems, such as appointment scheduling, patient admissions, and claims processing.	Uses ERP to connect various healthcare services, enabling seamless data flow between departments and supporting strategic decision-making.
Technology Used	Core ERP modules tailored for healthcare (e.g., SAP, Oracle Healthcare, Infor) focusing on automation of administrative functions.	Integration of ERP with electronic health records (EHR), AI for predictive diagnostics, IoT for patient monitoring, and telehealth platforms.

Impact on Culture	Limited cultural change; focuses on improving back-office operations without altering clinical workflows significantly.	Drives a shift towards a more collaborative, patient-centered approach, with an emphasis on data-driven clinical decisions and personalized care.
Timeframe	Shorter deployment cycles, often focused on automating specific administrative processes within healthcare ERP modules.	Longer timelines due to integration with other digital health technologies and transformation of care delivery models.
Challenges	Requires careful system configuration, staff training, and adherence to healthcare compliance and data privacy regulations.	Involves complex integration challenges, high costs, and requires substantial change management, especially in clinical and patient-facing areas.

Added Value	Reduces administrative burdens, improves compliance, and enhances financial management, leading to cost savings in non-clinical areas.	Creates value by improving patient outcomes, enhancing care delivery speed, and opening opportunities for new healthcare services.
Strategic Alignment	ERP aligns with goals of operational efficiency, regulatory compliance, and cost control.	ERP becomes a strategic enabler for long-term goals like improving patient care, expanding digital health services, and enhancing clinical quality.
Customer-Centricity	Primarily focuses on improving administrative efficiency with indirect benefits to patient care.	Directly impacts patient care by enabling faster access to information, personalized treatment plans, and improved overall patient satisfaction.

Innovation Capability	Low; improves existing administrative processes without significantly impacting clinical care models.	High; ERP integrates with innovative healthcare technologies to support new treatment approaches, predictive analytics, and digital care models.
Employee Impact	May reduce administrative workload but requires training for staff to manage and utilize ERP systems effectively.	Encourages upskilling of clinical staff, creating roles focused on health informatics, data analysis, and digital patient engagement.
Scalability	Scalable within administrative domains but may require new modules or customizations for broader clinical integration.	Highly scalable, supporting the expansion of digital health initiatives, remote care, and integration with new healthcare technologies.

| Risk Management | Minimizes operational risks by standardizing processes and enhancing data accuracy, particularly in compliance reporting. | Balances clinical and operational risks, requiring robust data security measures, change management, and patient data privacy protections. |

6. Cloud Computing

- **What It Is**: Storing and managing data on remote servers accessed over the internet rather than local systems.

- **Why It's Game-Changing**: Cloud computing offers healthcare organizations scalable storage for data, which is crucial as they handle massive amounts of information. It also enables better data security, collaboration, and cost savings.

Below is an *indicative* table that incorporates healthcare technology vendors, indicating whether they are cloud providers or healthcare-specific application providers, and mapping them to their respective healthcare use cases.

Category	AWS	Google Cloud	MS Azure	Oracle Cloud	IBM Cloud	SAP	Other Vendors	Healthcare Use Cases
IaaS/Compute	EC2	Compute Engine	Virtual Machines	OCI Compute	Virtual Servers	SAP HANA Enterprise Cloud	Alibaba Cloud, Tencent Cloud	Hosting health data applications, running EHR systems

Category	AWS	Google Cloud	MS Azure	Oracle Cloud	IBM Cloud	SAP	Other Vendors	Healthcare Use Cases
Containers	ECS, EKS	GKE, Cloud Run	AKS, Container Instances	Container Engine for Kubernetes	Kubernetes Service	SAP Cloud Platform	Dedalus Group	Deploying scalable healthcare microservices
PaaS	Elastic Beanstalk	App Engine	App Service	Application Development	Cloud Foundry	SAP Business Technology Platform	Athenahealth, NextGen Healthcare	Building custom healthcare apps
Storage	S3, EBS, Glacier	Persistent Disk, Filestore	Azure Blob Storage, Files	Object Storage, Archive	Cloud Object Storage	SAP Data Warehouse Cloud	Alibaba Cloud (Object Storage), Tencent Cloud (Cloud Storage)	Archiving patient records, enabling compliance
Database	RDS, DynamoDB	Cloud SQL, Firestore	Azure Cosmos DB	Exadata, Autonomous DB	Db2, Databases for Elasticsearch	SAP HANA	Epic (non-cloud EHR), Cerner (cloud EHR), InterSystems Iris, Change Healthcare	Managing EHR data, enabling analytics, supporting FHIR data
AI/ML	SageMaker, Comprehend	Vertex AI, Cloud Vision	AI Services	Oracle AI	Watson AI	SAP AI	NVIDIA Clara, Palantir Foundry	AI-driven diagnostics, predictive analytics, clinical decision support
Security	IAM, Cognito, GuardDuty	Cloud IAM, Identity Platform	Azure Active Directory	Identity & Access Management	IAM, App ID	SAP Identity Management	Change Healthcare (Interoperability & Security Solutions)	Ensuring patient data security, meeting HIPAA compliance

Category	AWS	Google Cloud	MS Azure	Oracle Cloud	IBM Cloud	SAP	Other Vendors	Healthcare Use Cases
IoT	IoT Core, IoT Analytics	IoT Core	IoT Hub, IoT Central	IoT Cloud Service	Watson IoT	SAP IoT	Philips Healthcare (IoT devices), Siemens Healthineers (IoT), Alibaba Cloud IoT	Remote patient monitoring, device integration for real-time care
Healthcare Apps	Amazon Health Lake	Google Cloud for Healthcare	Azure Health Data Services	Oracle Health	Watson Health	SAP Health	Meditech, Allscripts, GE HealthCare, Redox	EHR systems, population health, interoperability, patient engagement
Telemedicine	Amazon Chime SDK	Google Cloud and Vertex AI, fitbit	Teams and Azure IoT	Oracle Health portfolio	Watson Health	N/A	Teladoc Health, Amwell (telemedicine platforms)	Remote consultations, chronic care management
Genomics	AWS Genomics CLI	Google Cloud Genomics and its Deep Variant AI tool	MS Genomics	OCI + NVIDIA	IBM Watson Health and Cloud Pak for Data	SAP HANA Cloud and Datasphere	Illumina (Cloud Genomics), NVIDIA Clara (Genomics AI)	Genomic data storage, AI-driven analysis
Interoperability	Health Lake + FHIR Works	FHIR API support in Google Cloud	Azure Healthcare APIs + IoMT	Oracle Cerner + FHIR	IBM Cloud Paks for Data + Watson Health	SAP BTP + FHIR	InterSystems, Redox, HealthShare	Data exchange and integration across healthcare systems

Category	AWS	Google Cloud	MS Azure	Oracle Cloud	IBM Cloud	SAP	Other Vendors	Healthcare Use Cases
VR/AR	AWS Sumerian	Google VR SDK	Microsoft HoloLens + Azure Spatial	Collaboration with AvaSure's AI virtual concierge	IBM Watson Media	SAP's collaboration with **Microsoft HoloLens** and the **SAP Fiori launchpad**	Unity, Unreal Engine, Osso VR, FundamentalVR	Healthcare training, surgery simulations

3.4: Benefits of Digital Transformation in Healthcare

Improved Patient Care and Experience

When data is readily available, healthcare providers can make more accurate diagnoses, prescribe better treatments, and provide faster care. Digital tools like patient portals allow patients to access their own health records, schedule appointments, and communicate with providers directly, enhancing their overall experience.

Cost Savings and Efficiency

Digital transformation reduces time spent on administrative tasks. For example, AI-powered systems can help automate patient registration, billing, and claims processing, freeing up time and reducing costs. This helps providers focus more on direct patient care.

Enhanced Data Security and Compliance

With digital tools come new, secure ways to manage and store sensitive patient information. Advanced encryption and cybersecurity measures protect patient data from unauthorized access, helping healthcare providers comply with regulations like HIPAA (Health Insurance Portability and Accountability Act in the U.S.) and GDPR (General Data Protection Regulation in Europe).

Expanding Access to Healthcare

Digital health tools, like telemedicine, break down geographical barriers, enabling patients in remote areas to connect with healthcare providers. Digital solutions can also facilitate public health monitoring and emergency response, improving overall community health.

3.5: Technology vendors, system integrators, and consulting firms worldwide

The healthcare industry is supported by numerous technology vendors, system integrators, and consulting firms worldwide. These companies vary by geographic representation, as certain firms have stronger presences in specific regions. Below is an overview of key players categorized by geographic regions.

1. North America (USA and Canada)

Technology Vendors

- **Epic Systems**: Leading provider of electronic health record (EHR) software, widely used across U.S. hospitals.
- **Cerner (now part of Oracle Health)**: A major EHR provider offering comprehensive health IT solutions.
- **GE Healthcare**: Provides medical imaging, monitoring, and health cloud solutions.

- **IBM Watson Health**: Specializes in AI-driven healthcare solutions, analytics, and data management.
- **Microsoft Healthcare Cloud**: Offers cloud and AI services for healthcare operations, data sharing, and patient management.

System Integrators

- **Accenture**: Provides digital transformation services including AI, analytics, cloud computing, and system integration tailored to healthcare.
- **Cognizant**: Delivers healthcare IT solutions focusing on digital strategy, AI, and integrated health systems.
- **Deloitte**: Integrates technology solutions for EHRs, data analytics, and healthcare IT architecture.

Consulting Firms

- **McKinsey & Company**: Offers consulting on digital transformation, operational improvement, and innovation in healthcare.
- **Bain & Company**: Focuses on healthcare strategy, IT transformation, and digital health initiatives.
- **The Advisory Board Company**: Specializes in healthcare consulting, including digital health strategies and operational effectiveness.

2. Europe (Germany, UK, France, and Nordics)

Technology Vendors

- **Siemens Healthineers (Germany)**: Focuses on medical imaging, diagnostics, and healthcare IT solutions.
- **Philips Healthcare (Netherlands)**: Provides health informatics, medical devices, and digital health solutions.

- **Dedalus (Italy)**: A leading EHR and healthcare IT solution provider in Europe, specializing in clinical and hospital management systems.
- **Tunstall Healthcare (UK)**: Offers remote monitoring, telecare, and telehealth solutions.

System Integrators

- **Capgemini (France)**: Provides digital transformation services, focusing on cloud, IoT, and AI-based healthcare solutions.
- **Atos (France)**: Specializes in healthcare IT infrastructure, EHR integration, and telemedicine solutions.
- **DXC Technology (UK)**: Offers healthcare system integration, analytics, and health IT consulting.

Consulting Firms

- **Roland Berger (Germany)**: Advises on healthcare innovation, digital health strategies, and operational efficiency.
- **PwC Health Industries (UK)**: Offers consulting services on health technology implementation, EHR integration, and healthcare management.
- **KPMG Healthcare Advisory (UK)**: Focuses on healthcare transformation, IT systems, and operational improvement in healthcare organizations.

3. Asia-Pacific (India, China, Japan, and Australia)

Technology Vendors

- **Ping An Good Doctor (China)**: A major digital health platform providing telemedicine and health monitoring services.
- **Nihon Kohden (Japan)**: Offers medical electronics and healthcare IT solutions for monitoring and diagnostics.

- **MediBuddy (India)**: Provides telemedicine, diagnostics, and healthcare IT services in India.
- **Telstra Health (Australia)**: Focuses on digital health services, telemedicine platforms, and patient data management.

System Integrators

- **Tata Consultancy Services (TCS) (India)**: Provides system integration for healthcare IT, AI, and data management services.
- **Wipro (India)**: Specializes in healthcare IT services, including EHR implementation, cloud computing, and analytics.
- **Fujitsu (Japan)**: Offers healthcare IT solutions, including system integration, AI-powered diagnostics, and cloud-based services.

Consulting Firms

- **Ernst & Young (EY) (Australia)**: Offers healthcare advisory services focusing on digital health transformation, technology implementation, and operational efficiency.
- **Deloitte Consulting (China)**: Focuses on healthcare IT strategy, digital health, and EHR system integration.
- **PwC Healthcare Advisory (India)**: Provides healthcare consulting with an emphasis on health IT, operational transformation, and digital strategy.

4. Middle East and Africa (MEA)

Technology Vendors

- **CureMD (Middle East)**: Provides cloud-based EHR and practice management solutions.
- **Carestream Health (South Africa)**: Focuses on medical imaging, healthcare IT, and radiology services.

- **Vezeeta (Middle East & Africa)**: A healthcare technology company providing telehealth, booking, and digital health services.

System Integrators

- **Gulf Business Machines (GBM) (Middle East)**: Provides IT solutions and system integration for healthcare, focusing on digital infrastructure and cloud computing.
- **Dimension Data (Africa)**: Specializes in healthcare IT systems, cloud computing, and data integration for hospitals and healthcare providers.
- **Saudi Telecom Company (STC) (Middle East)**: Focuses on healthcare IT integration, telemedicine solutions, and data management.

Consulting Firms

- **PwC Middle East Health Industries**: Offers healthcare consulting focused on digital transformation, EHR implementation, and healthcare analytics.
- **McKinsey & Company (Africa)**: Provides strategic consulting on healthcare innovation, operational efficiency, and IT systems.
- **Boston Consulting Group (Middle East)**: Advises on healthcare digital transformation, technology adoption, and healthcare management.

5. Latin America

Technology Vendors

- **Totvs (Brazil)**: A leading provider of healthcare management software and digital solutions for hospitals and clinics.

- **Pixeon (Brazil)**: Specializes in healthcare IT systems, including EHR, telemedicine, and clinical management software.
- **Prontmed (Brazil)**: Provides EHR solutions and data management services for healthcare providers.

System Integrators
- **Stefanini (Brazil)**: Offers IT services and system integration for healthcare, focusing on digital solutions and data analytics.
- **Everis (Spain, Latin America)**: Specializes in healthcare IT integration, digital transformation, and data management in Latin America.

Consulting Firms
- **PwC Latin America**: Focuses on healthcare advisory, digital health solutions, and operational improvement.
- **Deloitte (Latin America)**: Provides consulting on digital health initiatives, IT systems integration, and data analytics.

3.6: Challenges in Implementing Digital Transformation

1. High Costs of Implementation

Healthcare providers need to invest in new systems, software, and staff training to implement digital tools effectively. Small hospitals or clinics may find it hard to afford these costs, creating a barrier to digital transformation.

2. Data Privacy and Security Concerns

As healthcare data moves online, protecting it becomes a challenge. Cybersecurity threats like data breaches and ransomware attacks put sensitive patient information at risk. Healthcare providers must invest in strong security measures to safeguard this data.

3. Resistance to Change

Adopting new technology can be intimidating for staff who are used to traditional methods. Training programs, support systems, and leadership encouragement are essential to help healthcare workers embrace these changes.

4. Interoperability Issues

One of the biggest challenges is ensuring that different digital systems—like EHRs, lab systems, and imaging software—can communicate with each other. Interoperability is critical for a smooth flow of patient information but often requires overcoming compatibility and standardization issues.

Chapter 4: Intermediate Applications of Digital Technologies

As healthcare takes a bold leap into the digital age, it's no longer just about storing patient data electronically. It's about leveraging advanced technologies to deliver smarter, faster, and more personalized care. In this chapter, we'll explore the powerful tools that are reshaping healthcare, diving into real-world applications, success stories, and challenges.

4.1: Data Analytics and Decision Support Systems

The Power of Big data in healthcare

Imagine a world where a hospital knows which patients are at risk of complications before they even occur. This isn't science fiction—it's the power of big data. By analyzing vast amounts of information, healthcare providers can make decisions that save lives and resources.

- **Predictive Analytics**: Picture this: A patient's medical history, lifestyle data, and genetic profile are analyzed to predict their likelihood of developing diabetes. The care team intervenes early, changing the patient's life trajectory.

- **Personalized Medicine**: Treatments aren't "one-size-fits-all" anymore. Big data enables doctors to customize therapies based on individual factors, from genetics to lifestyle choices.

Clinical Decision Support Systems (CDSS)

Doctors have a lot on their plates. Enter CDSS, the digital sidekick every physician needs. These systems analyze patient data, cross-reference it with the latest research, and provide actionable recommendations, improving diagnostic accuracy and efficiency.

Example: A busy ER physician sees a patient with vague symptoms. CDSS analyzes the data and suggests possible diagnoses, flagging a rare but critical condition the doctor hadn't considered.

Case Study: Reducing Hospital Readmissions with Data Analytics

A major healthcare network used data analytics to identify high-risk patients before discharge. They implemented personalized follow-up plans, reducing readmissions by 15% within six months. This initiative saved millions and improved patient satisfaction.

4.2: Artificial Intelligence (AI) and Machine Learning (ML)

AI and ML: The Healthcare Revolution

AI isn't just for tech enthusiasts—it's transforming medicine in ways that feel almost magical. These technologies help doctors diagnose diseases faster, researchers discover drugs quicker, and patients access care more conveniently.

Digital transformation in healthcare leverages AI, data analytics, and automation to revolutionize patient care, optimize operations, and improve clinical outcomes. Below is an updated table summarizing each technology, its function, and its relevance to healthcare transformation use cases, along with added insights into ethical considerations, patient engagement, and emerging applications.

Technology	Function	Healthcare Use Cases
BChain (Blockchain)	A decentralized and distributed ledger technology.	Secure patient data sharing, drug traceability, managing medical records, ensuring data integrity, and patient consent management.
API (Application Programming Interface)	A set of rules allowing software applications to interact.	Interoperability between healthcare systems, EHR integration, telehealth platforms, and IoT device connectivity.
RPA (Robotic Process Automation)	Automates repetitive and rule-based tasks.	Appointment scheduling, billing, claims processing, administrative tasks, and enhancing workflow efficiency.
OCR (Optical Character Recognition)	Extracts text from images or scanned documents.	Digitizing patient records, automating data entry, processing medical forms, and reading prescriptions.
DWH (Data Warehousing)	A centralized repository for storing and consolidating diverse data sources.	Integrating clinical, operational, and patient data for analytics, reporting, and improving care coordination.
ML (Machine Learning)	Enables computers to learn from data and improve performance over time.	Predictive analytics for patient outcomes, personalized treatment recommendations, and risk stratification.

Technology	Function	Healthcare Use Cases
RNN (Recurrent Neural Network)	Designed for sequential data processing, especially time-series information.	Predicting patient deterioration, analyzing ECG and EEG data, and forecasting disease progression.
SVM (Support Vector Machines)	Used for classification and regression by finding hyperplanes between data.	Disease diagnosis, medical image classification, and patient segmentation for tailored interventions.
K-NN (K-Nearest Neighbors)	Classifies data points by identifying the closest neighbors in data.	Medical image analysis, patient risk assessment, and drug efficacy prediction, enhancing diagnostics.
TKN (Tokenization)	Replaces sensitive information with symbols or tokens.	Protecting patient data in EHRs, enhancing privacy in healthcare data exchange, and secure transactions.
PCA (Principal Component Analysis)	Reduces the dimensionality of data to reveal key variables.	Identifying key health indicators, feature extraction from medical imaging, and clustering patient data.
DL (Deep Learning)	Neural networks that learn patterns in data through multiple layers.	Medical imaging analysis, genomics, drug discovery, natural language processing in clinical notes, and precision medicine.

Technology	Function	Healthcare Use Cases
GAN (Generative Adversarial Network)	Neural networks that create realistic data through adversarial training.	Synthetic data generation, enhancing medical imaging, augmenting training data for AI models, and simulating clinical trials.
Naive Bayes	Classification based on probability distributions and feature independence.	Disease prediction, patient classification, and sentiment analysis of patient feedback to improve care.
CL (Clustering)	Groups similar data points based on shared characteristics.	Patient segmentation, identifying disease subtypes, grouping similar clinical cases, and personalized treatments.
Epoch	A complete cycle through the dataset during training of neural networks.	Optimizing AI models for medical diagnosis, treatment planning, and continuous learning in clinical settings.
K-M (K-Means Clustering)	Organizes data into clusters based on similarity and distances.	Grouping patients by symptoms, disease progression, and treatment responses, aiding in personalized care.

Technology	Function	Healthcare Use Cases
ASR (Automatic Speech Recognition)	Converts spoken language into text.	Transcribing doctor-patient conversations, automating clinical documentation, and enhancing voice-command systems in healthcare.
GPT (Generative Pre-trained Transformer)	Language models that perform a broad range of text-based tasks.	Automating clinical note generation, patient communication, summarizing medical literature, and supporting decision-making.
TTS (Text-to-Speech)	Converts written text into spoken language.	Assisting visually impaired patients, creating interactive patient education materials, and improving telehealth experiences.
LLM (Large Language Model)	Trained on extensive text data to understand and generate human-like text.	Patient consultation chatbots, summarizing clinical reports, and providing decision support to clinicians.
NLP (Natural Language Processing)	Enables computers to interpret, understand, and generate human language.	Extracting information from clinical notes, enhancing EHRs, analyzing patient feedback, and automating report generation.

Additional Areas of Impact in Healthcare Digital Transformation

1. **Ethical Considerations and Data Privacy:**
   - **Relevance**: Integrating AI in healthcare involves managing sensitive health data, requiring technologies like Blockchain, Tokenization, and APIs to ensure secure data handling, patient consent, and compliance with regulations like HIPAA and GDPR.
   - **Use Case**: Blockchain can secure data exchanges, manage patient consent digitally, and protect against unauthorized access, while Tokenization ensures patient privacy during data analysis.

2. **Patient Engagement and Experience**:
   - **Relevance**: Technologies like TTS, ASR, and chatbots powered by GPT and LLM improve patient engagement by providing accessible and personalized communication, enhancing the patient experience and adherence to care plans.
   - **Use Case**: Virtual health assistants can provide patients with 24/7 support, answer questions about their conditions, schedule appointments, and offer medication reminders, improving overall patient satisfaction.

3. **AI in Clinical Decision Support (CDS):**
   - **Relevance**: AI models, especially ML, NLP, and GPT, enhance clinical decision support by analyzing vast amounts of data to provide insights, recommendations, and predictive alerts for patient care.

- **Use Case**: AI-driven CDS tools can alert doctors to potential adverse drug interactions, recommend personalized treatment plans, and help identify patients at risk of complications.

4. **Real-Time Monitoring and IoT Integration**:

    - **Relevance**: AI integration with IoT devices and wearables allows continuous patient monitoring, real-time health data analysis, and early intervention, particularly in chronic disease management.

    - **Use Case**: Wearable devices equipped with ML algorithms can track vital signs, alert healthcare providers of abnormalities, and enable remote patient management, reducing hospital visits.

5. **Digital Twins in Healthcare**:

    - **Relevance**: Digital twins simulate virtual models of patients or clinical environments, using ML, DL, and data analytics to predict outcomes, optimize treatments, and improve operational efficiency.

    - **Use Case**: A digital twin of a patient can simulate how they might respond to different treatments, allowing for personalized care planning and risk assessment before actual implementation.

6. **AI in Genomics and Precision Medicine**:

    - **Relevance**: DL, GANs, and ML play critical roles in genomics by analyzing complex genetic data, identifying mutations, and assisting in the development of targeted therapies.

- **Use Case**: AI-driven genomics can help identify genetic predispositions to diseases, enabling personalized medicine approaches that match treatments to an individual's genetic profile.

7. **Integration of AI with Robotic Surgery and Rehabilitation**:
   - **Relevance**: AI supports precision in robotic-assisted surgeries and personalized rehabilitation programs, enhancing patient outcomes through minimally invasive procedures and tailored recovery plans.
   - **Use Case**: AI-powered robots can assist surgeons in delicate operations, while AI-driven rehabilitation systems provide customized exercise regimens based on patient progress.

8. **Natural Language Generation (NLG)**:
   - **Relevance**: Extending NLP capabilities, NLG generates human-readable reports and documentation, turning complex clinical data into understandable formats for patients and healthcare providers.
   - **Use Case**: NLG can automate the generation of patient summaries, discharge notes, and personalized health recommendations, saving clinicians time and reducing administrative workload.

4.3: Mobile Health (mHealth) and Wearable Devices

The Rise of mHealth

Mobile health apps and wearables like Fitbit or Apple Watch are turning patients into active participants in their care. From managing chronic conditions to tracking fitness goals, these tools empower individuals to take control of their health.

- **Wearables**: These devices monitor everything from heart rate to oxygen levels, providing real-time insights into a patient's health.
- **Self-Management**: Chronic disease patients can use apps to log symptoms, track medications, and communicate with their care teams seamlessly.

Ethical Concerns

Who owns the data collected by wearables? How secure is it? These are questions we must answer as mHealth becomes more integrated into care.

Case Study: Wearables and Heart Health

A healthcare provider introduced wearables for heart patients, tracking vital signs and sending alerts when abnormalities were detected. ER visits dropped by 20%, proving the value of wearable tech in proactive care.

4.4: Cybersecurity in Healthcare

The Growing Threat of Cyberattacks

As healthcare goes digital, cyber threats loom large. From ransomware attacks to phishing scams, hospitals are increasingly targeted. Protecting sensitive patient data isn't just a technical issue—it's a moral one.

- **Common Threats**: Ransomware locks hospital systems, phishing scams trick employees, and insiders sometimes misuse access.
- **Solutions**: Multi-factor authentication, encryption, and regular cybersecurity training can significantly reduce risks.

Regulations and Compliance

Regulations like HIPAA in the U.S. and GDPR in Europe are designed to protect patient data. Compliance isn't optional—it's the foundation of trust.

Case Study: The WannaCry Cyberattack

In 2017, a ransomware attack paralyzed the UK's National Health Service, delaying surgeries and compromising patient care. This wake-up call led to massive investments in cybersecurity infrastructure across healthcare systems.

Chapter 5: Advanced Digital Transformation Solutions

5.1: Internet of Medical Things (IoMT)

The **Internet of Medical Things (IoMT)** refers to the interconnected network of medical devices and sensors that collect, transmit, and analyze patient data in real time. By bridging the gap between patients and providers, IoMT is revolutionizing healthcare delivery, improving outcomes for both acute and chronic conditions.

What is IoMT?

- IoMT devices include **smart inhalers, connected pacemakers, wearable ECG monitors**, and **glucose sensors**. These devices collect data continuously, providing healthcare providers with actionable insights.
- **Smart Inhalers**: Monitor asthma patients' adherence and environmental triggers in real-time.
- **Connected Pacemakers**: Transmit heart rhythm data to cardiologists, enabling proactive care and device adjustments remotely.

Using IoMT in Hospitals and Home Care

1. **Hospitals**:
   - IoMT devices like **smart IV pumps** and **connected beds** monitor vital signs and optimize resource utilization.
   - Examples include sensors tracking post-operative recovery or reducing risks in ICU environments by detecting early signs of deterioration.

2. **Home Care**:
   - Devices such as **wearable health trackers** or **home-based continuous glucose monitors** allow patients with chronic diseases to manage conditions effectively.
   - Home IoMT minimizes hospital readmissions, reducing costs and improving convenience.

Regulatory and Data Integration Challenges

- **Interoperability**: Diverse IoMT devices often lack standardized communication protocols, limiting seamless data sharing.
- **Data Privacy**: IoMT generates vast amounts of sensitive health data, raising concerns about **HIPAA compliance** and cybersecurity vulnerabilities.
- **Regulatory Issues**: Strict requirements for device approval and concerns about liability when IoMT devices fail hinder faster adoption.

Case Study: IoMT-Enabled Devices in Post-Operative Care

- A hospital in **Singapore** implemented IoMT wearables for patients recovering from surgery. These devices monitored vital signs and flagged abnormalities in real-time, reducing post-op complications by 30%.
- **Result**: Fewer hospital stays, faster recoveries, and lower costs.

5.2: Blockchain in Healthcare

Blockchain is a decentralized, tamper-proof digital ledger technology with immense potential to transform healthcare. It ensures transparency, enhances security, and improves efficiency in managing health data.

How Blockchain Enhances Data Security

- **Data Security**: Blockchain's distributed nature ensures that health records are resistant to tampering or unauthorized changes.
- **Patient Consent Management**: Patients can control who accesses their records through permission-based access using **smart contracts**.

Decentralized Health Records

- Traditional centralized records are prone to breaches; blockchain decentralizes data storage, increasing transparency.
- **Example**: **MedRec**, a blockchain-based EHR system, enables patients and providers to securely share data without intermediaries.

The Role of Smart Contracts

- **Automated Agreements**: Smart contracts facilitate secure, transparent, and efficient transactions between providers and payers.
- **Example**: A smart contract can automate insurance claims, ensuring timely and accurate payments based on pre-defined criteria.

Case Study: Blockchain in Medical Supply Chains

- In **Estonia**, a pilot blockchain program tracked the origin and authenticity of medical supplies during COVID-19, reducing counterfeit risks and improving logistics.
- **Impact**: Streamlined processes and enhanced trust across stakeholders.

5.3: Robotic Process Automation (RPA) and Robotics

Robotics and **Robotic Process Automation (RPA)** are transforming healthcare by automating repetitive tasks and enhancing surgical precision.

Introduction to RPA in Healthcare

- RPA tools automate routine administrative tasks like **medical billing, appointment scheduling,** and **claims processing**.
- **Example**: An RPA system at a U.S. hospital automated patient intake forms, saving 20 hours of manual work per week.

Surgical Robots

- **Precision**: Surgical robots like the **da Vinci Surgical System** enable minimally invasive surgeries, reducing recovery times and improving outcomes.
- **Advancements**: Robotic systems can now assist with complex procedures such as **neurosurgery** and **cardiac interventions**.

Impact on Workforce and Efficiency

- **Administrative Efficiency**: By automating tasks, RPA reduces burnout and allows staff to focus on patient care.

- **Clinical Advancements**: Robotics reduces human error, enhancing patient safety during surgeries and diagnostics.

Case Study: Robotic Surgery at Johns Hopkins

- Johns Hopkins Hospital pioneered robotic-assisted surgery for prostate cancer. The **da Vinci robot** allowed for unparalleled precision, minimizing tissue damage and reducing recovery times.
- **Results**: Patients experienced a 20% faster recovery compared to traditional methods.

Chapter 6: Strategic Implementation of Digital Transformation in Healthcare

6.1: Building a Digital Transformation Strategy

Implementing a digital transformation strategy requires careful planning, clear goals, and a robust roadmap to align people, processes, and technology. This section explores the foundational steps healthcare organizations need to take to design and execute an effective strategy.

Assessing the Organization's Digital Maturity

- Before initiating any transformation, it's critical to assess the organization's current **digital maturity level**:

    - **Tools**: Utilize frameworks like the HIMSS Digital Health Indicator or custom maturity assessments.
    - **Key Areas to Evaluate**: EHR adoption, interoperability, IoT readiness, workforce digital literacy, and cybersecurity.
    - **Example**: Cleveland Clinic's maturity assessment identified gaps in patient engagement tools, leading to the development of its MyChart patient portal.

Setting Clear Goals and KPIs

- Establish **SMART goals** (Specific, Measurable, Achievable, Relevant, Time-bound) tied to strategic objectives:
    - **Goal**: Reduce hospital readmissions by 20% using telemedicine within 2 years.
    - **KPI**: Patient adherence rates for telehealth appointments, percentage reduction in readmission rates.

- Align goals with broader organizational objectives, such as improving patient outcomes and operational efficiency.

Building a Digital Transformation Roadmap

1. **Timelines**: Develop a phased approach—short-term (quick wins), medium-term, and long-term goals.
2. **Budgeting**: Allocate funds to priority projects while ensuring cost-effectiveness.
3. **Stakeholders**: Identify champions within leadership, IT, clinical, and patient communities.
    - **Example**: Cleveland Clinic's roadmap included rolling out telehealth pilots before scaling organization wide.

Case Study: Cleveland Clinic's Digital Transformation

- Cleveland Clinic's digital transformation strategy focused on enhancing patient engagement and operational efficiency:
    - Conducted a comprehensive digital readiness assessment.
    - Prioritized patient-facing technologies, including remote monitoring and telehealth.
    - Collaborated with tech vendors for seamless EHR integration.

- **Outcome**: 30% improvement in patient satisfaction and reduced wait times for consultations.

6.2: Leadership and Change Management

Successful digital transformation in healthcare relies heavily on strong leadership and effective change management. Leaders must cultivate a digital-first culture while addressing resistance to change.

Leadership Qualities for Driving Digital Transformation

- Visionary thinking: Leaders must anticipate future trends and align strategies accordingly.
- Collaboration: Engage stakeholders across all levels, from clinicians to administrative staff.
- Communication: Leaders should articulate the benefits of digital tools clearly and consistently.

Overcoming Resistance to Change

1. **Education**: Train staff on the value and usability of new technologies.
2. **Incentives**: Tie incentives to successful adoption, such as reduced workloads through automation.
3. **Support Systems**: Offer ongoing support through help desks, super-user programs, and regular updates.

Involving Patients and Staff

- Engage patients by including them in **pilot programs** and gathering feedback.

- Empower staff to co-create solutions, fostering a sense of ownership.
- Example: Mount Sinai actively involved nurses and doctors during its EHR rollout, ensuring workflows were optimized for clinical efficiency.

Case Study: Change Management at Mount Sinai

- During its EHR transition, Mount Sinai faced resistance due to perceived disruptions to workflows.
    - Leadership hosted town halls and focus groups to understand concerns.
    - Change management teams provided 24/7 support during the initial rollout.
- **Outcome**: Successful adoption within 12 months, with enhanced data accessibility and clinician satisfaction.

Chapter 7: Emerging Trends and the Future of Healthcare Digital Transformation

7.1: Precision Medicine and Genomics

Precision Medicine tailors treatment plans to an individual's genetic, environmental, and lifestyle factors. Digital tools and AI are enabling this transformative approach to healthcare.

What is Precision Medicine?
- Precision medicine uses **genetic sequencing**, **AI-driven analytics**, and patient data to provide targeted treatments.
    - Example: Oncology uses genetic markers to select the most effective cancer therapies.

Role of Genomics in Personalized Healthcare

- Genomics enables healthcare providers to identify risk factors and prevent diseases.
    - Example: BRCA1/BRCA2 genetic testing predicts breast cancer risk and informs preventive measures.
- **Genomics and Chronic Diseases**: Analyzing genetic predispositions helps manage conditions like diabetes or cardiovascular disease.

Impact of AI on Precision Medicine

- AI enhances the speed and accuracy of genomic analysis, enabling personalized therapies.

- **Case Study**: IBM Watson Oncology analyzed genetic data to recommend personalized cancer treatments, reducing diagnostic time by 60%.

7.2: Virtual Reality (VR) and Augmented Reality (AR) in healthcare

Immersive technologies like VR and AR are revolutionizing medical education, diagnostics, and therapy.

VR for Surgical Simulations and Training

- VR allows surgeons to practice complex procedures in a risk-free virtual environment.
    - Example: Stanford Medicine's VR surgical training programs reduced surgical errors by 25%.

AR for Patient Education and Diagnostics

- AR overlays digital information onto real-world visuals, aiding in diagnostics and patient understanding.
    - Example: AR headsets enable surgeons to visualize internal structures during procedures.

Future Potential of Immersive Tech

- Virtual wards and AR-enhanced telemedicine could redefine remote care.
- Collaborative VR platforms might allow surgeons across the globe to assist in real-time operations.

Case Study: VR for Pain Management in Children

- Children undergoing painful procedures at a pediatric hospital were given VR headsets to distract them with calming environments.
- **Outcome**: 50% reduction in perceived pain levels and lower reliance on painkillers.

7.3: 3D Printing and Bioprinting

3D printing technology is revolutionizing prosthetics, implants, and organ bioprinting.

How 3D Printing Works in Healthcare
- Layer-by-layer manufacturing creates precise medical devices tailored to individual needs.

Applications in Healthcare
- **Customized Prosthetics**: Affordable and personalized prosthetics for children and adults.
- **Dental Implants**: Tailored implants improve comfort and reduce manufacturing time.

Bioprinting and Organ Transplants
- **Bioprinting**: Uses biological materials to create functional tissues and organs.
  - Example: Researchers successfully bioprinted a miniature liver capable of performing metabolic functions.

Case Study: 3D-Printed Prosthetics for Children

- A global nonprofit developed low-cost, 3D-printed prosthetic limbs for children with limb differences.
- **Impact**: Improved mobility and self-esteem at a fraction of the cost of traditional prosthetics.

Chapter 8: The Quintuple Aim Framework and Its Role in Digital Transformation

Introduction

Healthcare systems worldwide face growing challenges, from rising costs to disparities in care. The *Quintuple Aim framework* provides a comprehensive vision to address these issues, focusing on five interconnected goals: improving population health, enhancing patient experience, reducing the cost of care, improving staff experience, and advancing health equity. By aligning digital transformation strategies with this framework, healthcare organizations can achieve sustainable improvements across all dimensions of care.

This chapter explores how the Quintuple Aim connects to healthcare digital transformation and demonstrates its practical application through tools, technologies, and strategies discussed in this book.

The Quintuple Aim and Digital Transformation Goals

Quintuple Aim	Aligned Digital Transformation Goals	Chapters & Tools from the Book
1. Improve Population Health	- Use predictive analytics for disease prevention. - Enable proactive interventions through IoT and wearable tech.	- **Chapter 4.1**: Data Analytics & Decision Support Systems (predictive tools). - **Chapter 5.1**: IoMT and chronic disease management devices.
2. Enhance Patient Experience	- Simplify access to care via telemedicine. - Improve communication using patient portals and mobile apps.	- **Chapter 4.3**: mHealth and Wearable Devices (empowering patients). - **Chapter 3.4**: Benefits of digital patient interaction tools.
3. Lower the Cost of Care	- Optimize resource allocation with AI and automation. - Reduce administrative burdens using ERP and RPA tools.	- **Chapter 5.3**: Robotic Process Automation (RPA) for efficiency. - **Chapter 3.5**: Addressing inefficiencies with ERP systems.
4. Improve Staff Experience	- Minimize administrative workloads with streamlined processes. - Implement workforce planning tools to reduce burnout.	- **Chapter 6.2**: Leadership and Change Management (building a supportive culture). - **Chapter 6.3**: Automation for administrative relief.

Quintuple Aim	Aligned Digital Transformation Goals	Chapters & Tools from the Book
5. Advance Health Equity	- Expand access to care with telemedicine. - Use AI to reduce bias and promote fair resource distribution.	- **Chapter 4.3**: Telemedicine and reaching underserved populations. - **Chapter 7.1**: Precision medicine tailored to marginalized groups.

Chapter 9: Aligning the Target Operating Model (TOM) with Healthcare's Digital Transformation Goals

Introduction

Healthcare systems around the world are facing a growing number of challenges, from rising costs to fragmented care and inefficiencies in service delivery. To address these, healthcare organizations need to rethink and redesign their operations. This is where the **Target Operating Model (TOM)** comes in. TOM is a blueprint for how an organization should be structured and how it should operate to achieve its goals effectively.

However, designing and implementing a TOM on its own isn't enough. It needs to align with broader, long-term goals for healthcare improvement, such as those outlined in the **Quintuple Aim Framework**. The Quintuple Aim sets the strategic goals that healthcare systems strive to achieve, including improving population health, enhancing patient experience, reducing the cost of care, improving staff well-being, and advancing health equity.

In this chapter, we'll explore how TOM and the Quintuple Aim framework work together. We'll look at their individual purposes, how they complement each other, and how they can be used in tandem to drive meaningful change in healthcare systems.

What is the Target Operating Model (TOM)?

The Target Operating Model (TOM) is a design tool that helps healthcare organizations determine **how to operate** in a way that improves efficiency, delivers better patient care, and aligns with long-term goals. It is focused on the "how" of healthcare delivery and involves:

1. **People**: Ensuring the right people are in the right roles with the right skills.
2. **Processes**: Streamlining workflows to eliminate inefficiencies and enhance patient care.
3. **Technology**: Leveraging digital tools like Electronic Health Records (EHR), AI, and IoMT to improve decision-making.
4. **Governance**: Creating clear decision-making frameworks and ensuring compliance with regulations.
5. **Performance Metrics**: Defining how success is measured through key performance indicators (KPIs).

TOM helps organizations re-engineer their operations to become more efficient, adaptive, and responsive to both current and future needs.

While the TOM focuses on **how** to redesign operations, the **Quintuple Aim** answers the **why**—why we're transforming healthcare systems in the first place. The Quintuple Aim outlines the broader strategic outcomes that organizations want to achieve, and TOM provides the operational foundation to make those outcomes a reality.

How TOM and the Quintuple Aim Work Together

TOM and the Quintuple Aim are two sides of the same coin. While the Quintuple Aim sets the long-term goals for healthcare systems, TOM ensures that the organization is structured and operates in a way that can achieve these goals.

Here's how they work together:

1. **TOM Makes the Quintuple Aim Achievable**: The Quintuple Aim outlines broad strategic objectives, but TOM breaks these down into actionable steps. For example, if one of the Quintuple Aim's goals is to **improve population health**, TOM can align processes and technology (like predictive analytics and IoMT) to support preventive care initiatives.

2. **TOM Aligns Operations with Strategic Outcomes**: Through well-defined processes, roles, and technologies, TOM ensures that all parts of the organization are working towards the Quintuple Aim goals. For instance, improving **staff well-being** through better work processes can reduce burnout, which directly contributes to the **Quintuple Aim's goal of improving staff experience**.

3. **Continuous Feedback Loop**: As TOM is implemented, it can provide feedback on progress toward the Quintuple Aim's goals. For example, TOM's focus on performance metrics (like reducing patient wait times or improving care coordination) can directly

measure the success of Quintuple Aim goals like **enhancing patient experience** or **reducing care costs**.

TOM and the Quintuple Aim: A Collaborative Approach

While TOM and the Quintuple Aim serve different purposes, they are not mutually exclusive. In fact, they **collaborate closely** to ensure that digital transformation in healthcare happens smoothly and effectively.

Here's how these two frameworks can work together in practice:

- **Improving Population Health**: TOM aligns healthcare workflows and technology to ensure preventive care is prioritized, and data analytics can be used to monitor and intervene early in chronic conditions.

- **Enhancing Patient Experience**: TOM ensures that care processes are streamlined and digital tools like patient portals or telehealth systems are integrated to give patients easier access to care.

- **Reducing the Cost of Care**: TOM focuses on operational efficiencies like automating administrative tasks with **Robotic Process Automation (RPA)**, which reduces costs and enhances the quality of patient care.

- **Improving Staff Well-Being**: By removing unnecessary administrative burdens through automation and improving workflows, TOM helps reduce burnout among healthcare workers, directly supporting staff well-being.

- **Advancing Health Equity**: TOM can integrate telemedicine, AI-driven diagnostics, and data analytics to ensure that underserved populations have access to care, which aligns with the Quintuple Aim's goal of improving health equity.

Mapping TOM to the Quintuple Aim Goals

Below is a table that shows how TOM components map to each of the **Quintuple Aim** goals and which chapters in the book support these connections.

Quintuple Aim Goal	TOM Component	Relevant Book Chapters	Tools/Examples
Improve Population Health	Processes, Technology	Chapter 4.1: Data Analytics & Decision Support, Chapter 5.1: IoMT	Predictive analytics, remote monitoring for chronic diseases
Enhance Patient Experience	People, Processes	Chapter 3.2: Key Technologies, Chapter 4.3: mHealth & Wearables	Telemedicine, patient portals, AI in diagnostics

Quintuple Aim Goal	TOM Component	Relevant Book Chapters	Tools/Examples
Reduce the Cost of Care	Processes, Technology, Metrics	Chapter 5.3: Robotic Process Automation, Chapter 3.5: ERP	Automation tools, AI-powered decision-making, supply chain optimization
Improve Staff Well-Being	People, Governance	Chapter 6.2: Leadership & Change Management	Leadership engagement, workflow optimization
Advance Health Equity	Technology, Governance	Chapter 7.1: Precision Medicine, Chapter 4.3: mHealth & Wearables	AI for reducing biases, telehealth for underserved populations

Conclusion

The **Target Operating Model (TOM)** and the **Quintuple Aim Framework** work hand-in-hand to create a healthcare system that is efficient, effective, and equitable. While the Quintuple Aim sets the strategic goals, TOM provides the operational structure needed to achieve these goals. By aligning both frameworks, healthcare organizations can drive sustainable transformation, leading to better outcomes for patients, providers, and communities.

In this chapter, we've seen how TOM provides the blueprint for operationalizing the strategic goals of the Quintuple Aim. In the next chapters, we'll dive deeper into the practical steps for implementing TOM in your organization and achieving these transformative healthcare outcomes.

Chapter 10: The Vision for a Unified Medical Database and Advanced Care Management System

Introduction

Imagine a healthcare system where every patient's medical history is accessible seamlessly across hospitals, clinics, and care providers, ensuring they receive the right care at the right time without unnecessary delays or repetition. A system where healthcare professionals can instantly access critical data to make life-saving decisions, and where researchers have access to aggregated, anonymized data to drive breakthroughs in medicine.

This vision—of a unified medical database and an advanced care management system—represents the future of healthcare. It promises to revolutionize the way care is delivered by prioritizing patient needs, improving collaboration across providers, and using data to support better decision-making and innovation. This chapter explores the foundational concepts, benefits, and considerations for implementing such a system on a national or regional scale.

Why a Unified Medical Database is Essential

In today's fragmented healthcare systems, patient data is often siloed across various providers and platforms, leading to inefficiencies, duplications, and missed opportunities for timely interventions. A unified medical database addresses these challenges by creating a single, secure, and comprehensive record for every patient, accessible by authorized healthcare professionals.

The key goals of such a system include:

1. **Creating Continuity of Care**

    By integrating all medical records, the system ensures that care providers have access to a complete patient history, reducing errors, unnecessary tests, and missed diagnoses.

2. **Promoting Collaboration**

    Seamless data exchange allows different providers such as hospitals, clinics, laboratories, and pharmacies to work together efficiently, improving overall care coordination.

3. **Enhancing Public Health**

    Aggregated and anonymized data from the system can be used for early detection of outbreaks, better management of chronic diseases, and data-driven policymaking to improve population health.

4. **Fostering Innovation**

   Researchers can leverage the data to accelerate medical discoveries, support clinical trials, and develop personalized treatment plans tailored to individual needs.

Core Features of an Advanced Care Management System

Building a system that achieves these goals requires a combination of cutting-edge technologies and well-designed workflows. Some of the essential components include:

1. **Unified Health Records**
   Every individual would have a comprehensive, longitudinal medical record that consolidates data from all interactions with the healthcare system. This record could include diagnostic reports, prescriptions, imaging, and even wearable device data, all stored securely and accessible in real time.

2. **Data Interoperability**
   The system must enable seamless communication between diverse healthcare platforms and software. Open standards for interoperability ensure that different systems can "talk" to each other, regardless of their vendor or origin.

3. **Personalized Insights Through AI and Analytics**
   Advanced analytics and artificial intelligence can process the vast amounts of data stored in the system to identify patterns, predict outcomes, and suggest interventions. For example, AI

tools could flag patients at high risk for complications or provide decision support to clinicians based on the latest medical research.

4. **Cloud-Based Infrastructure**
   A secure, scalable cloud infrastructure allows for the storage and processing of large volumes of data while ensuring accessibility from anywhere. Cloud systems also provide built-in compliance with data privacy regulations and support disaster recovery.

5. **Support for Clinical Research**
   By integrating clinical trial management tools, the system can support researchers in recruiting participants, monitoring trials, and analyzing outcomes, positioning the healthcare system as a leader in medical innovation.

Challenges to Overcome

While the benefits are compelling, building such a system comes with challenges that must be addressed through strategic planning and collaboration:

1. **Data Security and Privacy**
   Protecting sensitive health information is paramount. Strong cybersecurity measures, encryption, and role-based access controls are necessary to safeguard patient data from breaches or misuse.

2. **Interoperability Across Providers**
   Many healthcare providers use legacy systems that may not easily integrate with new technologies. Establishing common

data standards and protocols is critical to overcome these barriers.

3. **Workforce Adaptation**
   Healthcare professionals need to be trained to effectively use the new tools and workflows. Upskilling the workforce is essential for successful adoption and utilization of the system.

4. **Change Management**
   Introducing a system of this scale requires a cultural shift within healthcare organizations. Resistance to change must be managed through clear communication, leadership engagement, and gradual implementation.

5. **Financial Investment**
   Building and maintaining a unified medical database requires significant upfront investment, both in terms of technology and infrastructure. Demonstrating long-term cost savings and benefits can help secure the necessary funding.

Transformative Impact

The implementation of a unified medical database and care management system has the potential to deliver profound benefits:

1. **For Patients**
   - **Personalized Care**: Clinicians can tailor treatments based on the patient's complete medical history.

- **Better Access**: Patients can access their own medical records, schedule appointments, and communicate with providers more easily through integrated digital tools.

2. **For Healthcare Providers**

    - **Streamlined Workflows**: Automation of administrative tasks frees up time for direct patient care.
    - **Improved Decision-Making**: Providers have real-time access to the data and insights they need to deliver high-quality care.

3. **For Public Health**

    - **Early Detection**: Aggregated data can be used to predict and prevent disease outbreaks.
    - **Resource Optimization**: Analytics can help policymakers allocate resources more effectively, ensuring they are directed to where they are needed most.

4. **For Researchers and Innovators**

    - **Accelerated Discovery**: Access to a rich dataset enables breakthroughs in diagnostics, treatment, and medical devices.
    - **Collaboration**: Researchers across institutions can collaborate more effectively, sharing insights and findings.

A Collaborative Approach

The success of a unified medical database depends on collaboration among stakeholders, including healthcare providers, regulators, technology companies, and patients. Key principles for successful collaboration include:

- **Shared Vision**: Aligning all parties around common goals, such as improving care quality and equity.

- **Transparency**: Ensuring clear communication and accountability throughout the implementation process.

- **Standardization**: Establishing consistent protocols and metrics for data sharing and system performance.

A Future Built on Data

A unified medical database and care management system is not just a technical achievement; it represents a new paradigm for healthcare—one that puts patients at the center, empowers providers, and accelerates progress toward better health for all.

By addressing the challenges and embracing the opportunities, healthcare systems worldwide can pave the way for a future where data-driven care becomes the norm, delivering improved outcomes, greater efficiency, and a higher standard of care for everyone.

Chapter 11: Understanding HL7 and FHIR in Healthcare Interoperability

Introduction to HL7

Health Level Seven (HL7) is an international, non-profit organization that develops standards for the exchange, integration, sharing, and retrieval of electronic health information. HL7 standards enable different healthcare systems and applications—such as hospitals, laboratories, pharmacies, and insurance providers—to share and exchange critical data securely and efficiently.

The HL7 standard includes several versions:

- **HL7 V2**: The most widely used standard for healthcare messaging, enabling systems to send patient data and other health information.

- **HL7 V3**: An improvement over V2, HL7 V3 provides a more structured approach with better data modeling, though its complexity has limited adoption.

- **FHIR (Fast Healthcare Interoperability Resources)**: A more modern, flexible standard that is gaining traction, focusing on real-time data exchange via web technologies.

HL7 standards are crucial in enabling interoperability across healthcare systems, addressing challenges like fragmented data, and enhancing patient care and safety. However, due to evolving technology and changing needs, **FHIR** has become the new standard of choice, particularly for real-time and mobile applications.

HL7 V2 and V3: Legacy Messaging Systems

- **HL7 V2**: Developed in the late 1980s, HL7 V2 is still widely used today. It structures healthcare messages in a human-readable format, which makes it easier for healthcare professionals to implement. However, the complexity of V2's message structures, its reliance on different "versions," and the absence of a standardized approach to data exchange have been some of its limitations. Despite this, it remains essential in supporting hospital systems and lab applications across the globe.

- **HL7 V3**: Launched in the early 2000s, HL7 V3 aimed to bring more rigor and standardization to healthcare data exchange, but it faced adoption challenges due to its complexity and the steep learning curve required. V3's XML-based messaging format was more robust but also much harder to implement, leading to its slower uptake compared to V2.

FHIR: A Modern Approach to Interoperability

In response to the limitations of HL7 V2 and V3, **FHIR** was developed to provide a simpler, more adaptable solution to healthcare interoperability. First introduced in 2014, FHIR leverages modern web technologies like RESTful APIs, XML, and JSON to facilitate the exchange of health data.

Key Features of FHIR:

1. **RESTful APIs**: FHIR uses REST (Representational State Transfer) APIs to ensure that healthcare data can be retrieved or sent from systems in a lightweight, web-based manner. This enables real-time data access from multiple sources like EHRs, mobile apps, or wearable devices.

2. **Modular Resources**: FHIR breaks down healthcare data into "resources" (e.g., patients, observations, medications), each of which is independently structured and can be exchanged. This

modularity allows for flexible data sharing and makes it easier to integrate new systems and applications without needing to overhaul entire data structures.

3. **Interoperability**: FHIR supports major healthcare standards like **HL7 V2**, **V3**, and **CDA**, ensuring compatibility with legacy systems. Its support for existing data standards and the integration of APIs means that even older systems can communicate with newer, cloud-based applications.

4. **Mobile and Cloud Friendly**: FHIR's design makes it compatible with cloud-based services and mobile devices, which is critical for today's healthcare needs that demand mobility and remote access. This is especially useful for patient engagement and telemedicine.

FHIR Resources in Action

FHIR provides a set of core resources that can be used across various healthcare applications:

- **Patient Resource**: Contains demographic information about a patient.

- **Observation Resource**: Represents medical measurements or observations (e.g., vital signs, lab results).

- **Medication Resource**: Used to represent a medication prescription or administration event.

FHIR also supports **SMART on FHIR**, an extension that allows for easier integration of applications with electronic health systems like EHRs.

Example: **Apple Health** integrates FHIR to allow users to access their medical records and health data, enhancing patient engagement and empowering them to share their health data directly with providers.

HL7 vs. FHIR: A Comparison

Feature	HL7	FHIR
Technology	Uses older messaging protocols like XML	Uses modern web technologies like REST APIs, JSON, and XML
Complexity	Complex and rigid structure, steep learning curve	Simpler, modular structure with flexible data exchange
Real-Time Integration	Limited, requires heavy customization	Supports real-time data access and integration
Adoption	Widespread, especially V2 (legacy systems)	Increasingly adopted, especially for mobile and cloud-based solutions
Interoperability	Supports basic interoperability but lacks flexibility	Designed for high interoperability and modern app integration

FHIR's flexibility, ease of implementation, and support for real-time data exchange make it ideal for mobile health applications and cloud-based EHR solutions.

Benefits of FHIR in Healthcare

- **Improved Data Sharing**: FHIR simplifies the sharing of critical patient information between hospitals, labs, and pharmacies. Its standardized format ensures that all parties can understand the data.

- **Real-Time Access**: Healthcare professionals can access patient records immediately, improving diagnosis and treatment times. This is particularly important in urgent care scenarios.

- **Patient Empowerment**: FHIR enables patients to access and control their health data, which can improve engagement and adherence to treatment plans. Apps like **Apple Health** allow patients to monitor and share their health records with doctors.

- **Cost-Effective**: FHIR's use of RESTful APIs and modular resources means it is easier to implement, and scale compared to older HL7 versions, reducing both initial and long-term costs.

Challenges of FHIR and Future Considerations

While FHIR offers many benefits, it does face challenges:

- **Data Privacy and Security**: Protecting patient data is critical, and FHIR-based systems must ensure compliance with HIPAA, GDPR, and other data privacy regulations.

- **System Integration**: Many healthcare organizations still rely on legacy EHR systems, which may not be fully compatible with FHIR. Bridging this gap requires both time and investment.

- **Standardization of Resources**: Although FHIR standardizes a wide range of data resources, there is still work to be done to ensure that all healthcare data is captured in a standardized, interoperable way.

Despite these challenges, FHIR represents the future of healthcare interoperability, supporting the movement towards more integrated, patient-centred care.

Conclusion

FHIR is rapidly becoming the standard for healthcare data exchange. It solves many of the issues associated with older HL7 standards by offering a more modern, flexible, and real-time solution for interoperability. As healthcare continues to move towards more connected, cloud-based systems, FHIR will play a pivotal role in ensuring that data flows seamlessly between applications, systems, and providers, ultimately improving patient outcomes and advancing digital health innovation.

Chapter 12: ConsultCare: A Catalyst for Digital Healthcare Transformation

Introduction

In emergencies, every second matters. *ConsultCare* is a groundbreaking AI-powered platform that bridges critical gaps in emergency healthcare. It is the result of extensive research and insights gained during my certification at Harvard Medical School, where I deepened my understanding of healthcare innovation and digital transformation. This foundation enabled me to design a product that addresses one of the most pressing challenges in healthcare: fragmented and inaccessible patient information.

ConsultCare combines advanced artificial intelligence with robust data management to provide real-time emergency guidance. It ensures that patients, healthcare providers, and insurance companies have access to the right information at the right time, enabling faster and more accurate decisions when lives are on the line.

Inspired by the vision to revolutionize emergency care, *ConsultCare* embodies the principles of innovation, patient safety, and operational efficiency, offering a transformative solution for the future of healthcare.

The Problem

In Case of emergency and lifesaving situations, patient usually is not ready for that moment, weather the patient is in his own country or travelling, when an ambulance transfers the patient to the nearest emergency facility the medical staff working on this case has no pregiven information about this patient i.e. chronical diseases, heart conditions history echo's, previous surgeries, etc.

That's why in emergencies; patients often don't receive timely and accurate guidance due to fragmented or inaccessible health information. Key challenges include:

- **Fragmented Health Records**: Lack of unified access to Electronic Health Records (EHRs) leads to delays and misinformed decisions.
- **Limited Emergency Preparedness**: Patients and providers are often unprepared, especially during critical, life-threatening moments.

Impact: These gaps result in increased risks, delayed treatment, and suboptimal healthcare outcomes.

ConsultCare: The Solution

ConsultCare addresses these challenges by offering a comprehensive, AI-driven platform. Its core features include:

1. **Real-Time Emergency Guidance**: Provides instant treatment recommendations by analyzing patient history, EHRs, and symptoms.

2. **Comprehensive Data Integration**: Combines EHRs, local hospital conditions, and wearable tech data for a complete picture.

3. **Privacy and Security**: Ensures compliance with regulations through strong encryption, anonymization, and access controls.

4. **Predictive Analytics**: Identifies the best facility or treatment pathway based on the patient's current condition and medical history.

Unique Value Proposition

Unlike other solutions, *ConsultCare* focuses on:

- **Real-Time Response**: Tailored specifically for emergency care.
- **Comprehensive Data Handling**: Integrates diverse data types (e.g., EHRs, wearables, hospital statuses) to provide holistic insights.
- **Privacy and Bias Mitigation**: Strong emphasis on protecting patient data and minimizing AI bias.

ConsultCare Impact on Key Stakeholders

- The patient population, my solution will allow everyone to feel safe cause they have they universal consolidated EHR with them, that could save their lives and provide them with better opportunity for accurate diagnosis and treatment,
- The health care workers in general and specific the emergency workers, who can extract the EHR of the patient in seconds to know all the needed details about the patient which will allow them to better diagnose and treat the case, in a very speedy and more accurate way.
- The health care insurance companies will have better validation about the health care provider diagnosis and treatment once using this solution.

Model Structure

The below model shows the summary that outlines the essential steps for planning, developing, and maintaining ConsultCare AI solution for emergency healthcare

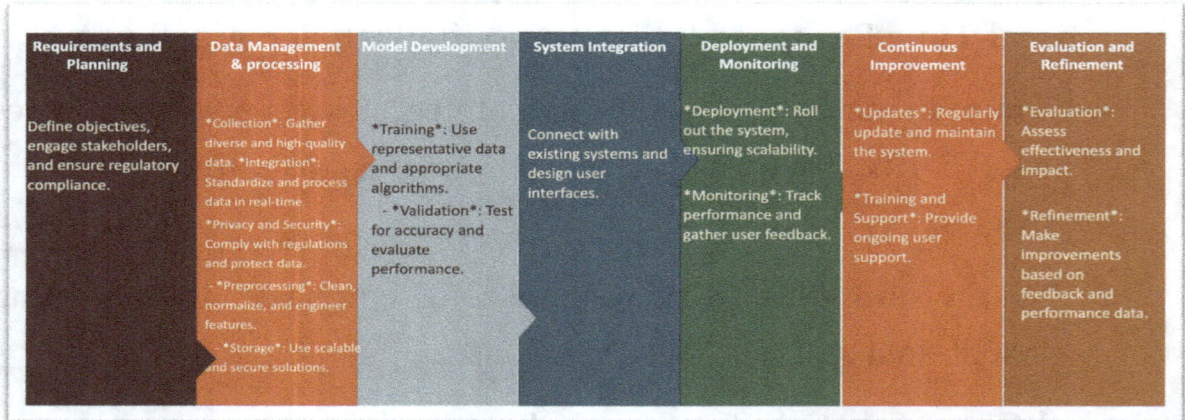

Data Strategy

The data needed to my AI system is mainly - EHR records, - Clinical test results in the last 3 to 6 months, - Latest medical reports in last 3 to 6 months, - Previous heart echo, MRIs etc.- Patient treatment preferences if any. More Data Types to consider: Genetic information or social factors (like income or living situation) that might affect health. Potential Problem: Bias: Data might not represent all populations equally.

Diagram below shows the data strategy implementation flow

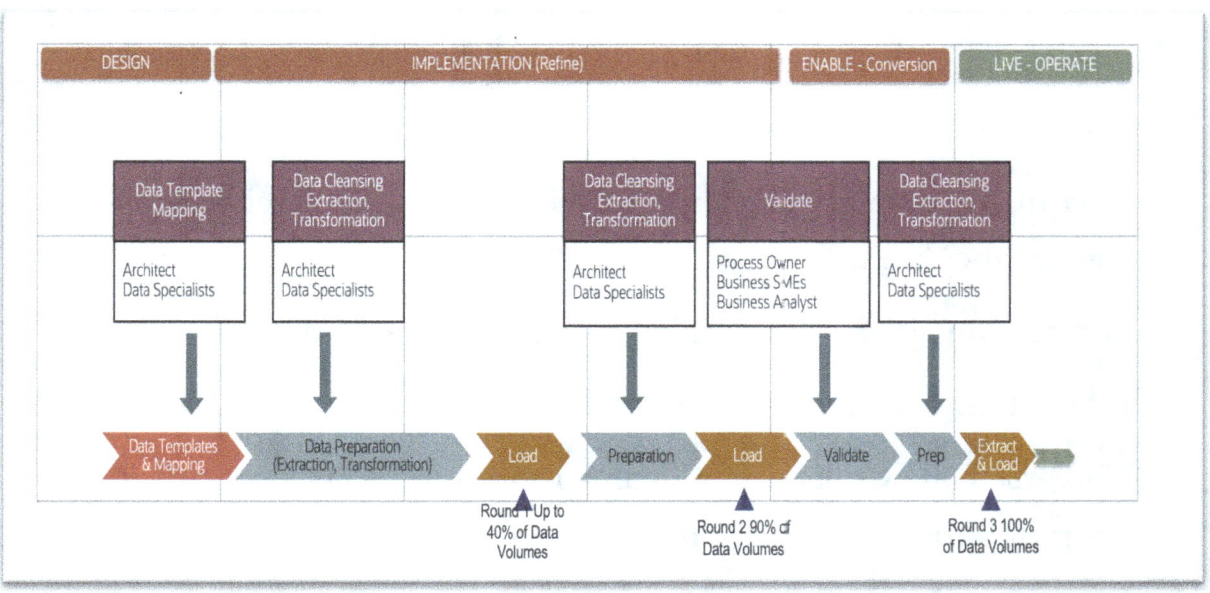

Implementation Strategy & Compliance

ConsultCare an AI Solution that connects with each branch, Integration with Existing Healthcare IT Systems, Continuous Evolution and Updates, Privacy and Compliance, Stakeholder Interaction

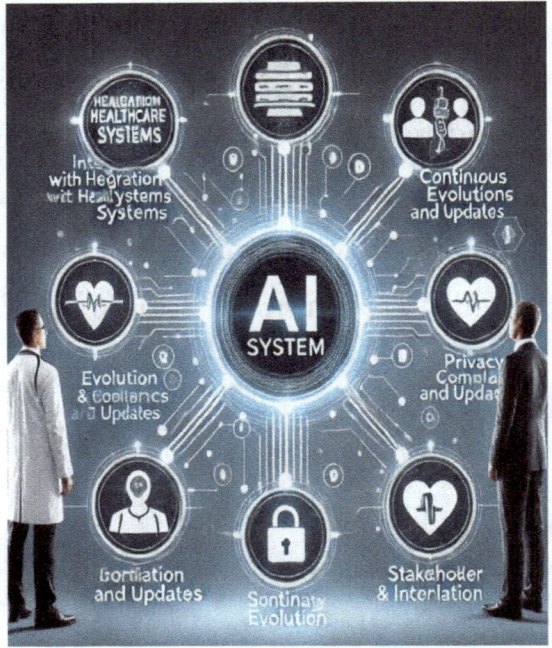

The potential regulatory implications for this system are mainly:

- Compliance with patient regulations and privacy.
- Acquiring a timely consent from the patient before check-in to the emergency unit.
- Protection against data leakage or cyber-attacks or theft.

How we will Manage these requirements:

- Diverse Data Collection: Ensures representation from various populations to minimize bias.
- Continuous Monitoring: Regularly checks for and addresses potential biases in AI predictions.

Patient Data Protection: Adheres to strict privacy regulations, including HIPAA compliance.

ConsultCare – Your Guarding Angel in emergencies

ConsultCare represents more than a product—it's a revolution in healthcare. By integrating advanced AI with robust data management and continuous improvement practices, *ConsultCare* paves the way for smarter, safer, and more efficient emergency care systems.

With its focus on real-time guidance, comprehensive data integration, and patient-centered innovation, *ConsultCare* is poised to transform how emergencies are managed globally.

"By integrating advanced AI with robust data management and continuous improvement practices, ConsultCare can revolutionize emergency response systems, ensuring faster, more accurate diagnoses and ultimately saving lives.

Together, lets lead the way in transforming emergency care with innovative technology"

Chapter 13: A Holistic Digital Transformation Roadmap

Introduction: Building the Future of Healthcare Together

Imagine a healthcare system where patients feel valued, staff love their work, and access to quality care is available to everyone, all while keeping costs in check. That's the vision of the Quintuple Aim—a framework that puts people and communities at the heart of transformation. But achieving these interconnected goals takes more than just adopting technology; it requires a thoughtful and unified plan.

This chapter is your guide to making it happen. Whether you're a leader, a tech enthusiast, or a healthcare professional, this roadmap will help you navigate the complex journey of digital transformation, with practical steps and inspiring real-world stories.

7-Step Roadmap to Healthcare Transformation

1. Start with a Clear Vision

Every great journey starts with knowing where you want to go. Define your goals and ask:

- How can we improve patient health and satisfaction?
- What would better support our staff?
- Where can we save costs without compromising quality?

Set measurable targets, like reducing hospital readmissions or improving access to care in underserved areas.

- **Inspiration**: Cleveland Clinic expanded telemedicine during COVID-19, meeting patient needs while improving satisfaction scores.

2. Build the Right Foundation

You can't transform healthcare without the right tools. Create a solid digital infrastructure by:

- Integrating systems like electronic health records (EHRs) and telemedicine platforms.
- Ensuring different tools can "talk" to each other (interoperability).
- Prioritizing cybersecurity to protect sensitive patient data.

Example: Mount Sinai Health System streamlined care by investing in interoperable systems, reducing silos between departments.

3. Focus on Preventing Problems

Why wait for issues to arise when you can prevent them? Use data to stay one step ahead:

- Predict who might be at risk of complications and provide timely interventions.
- Equip patients with wearable devices to track chronic conditions like diabetes or heart disease.

Success Story: Kaiser Permanente used analytics to identify at-risk patients, providing proactive care and improving community health.

4. Make Healthcare Simple and Human for Patients

Patients should feel like they're in control of their healthcare journey. Here's how:

- Offer easy access to appointments through mobile apps.
- Provide 24/7 support with chatbots and patient portals.
- Use plain language and intuitive designs to make technology accessible.

Inspiration: Mayo Clinic introduced an AI-powered chatbot to help patients with scheduling and FAQs, cutting waiting times and boosting satisfaction.

5. Save Time and Money with Smart Automation

Technology should work for you, not the other way around. Automate repetitive tasks like billing and scheduling to free up staff for what matters most—patient care.

- Use robotic process automation (RPA) to handle paperwork.
- Optimize supply chains with tools like ERP systems.

Example: Johns Hopkins Medicine used automation to cut procurement costs by 30%, freeing up resources for patient care.

6. Take Care of Your Team

Happy, supported staff lead to better care for everyone. Focus on reducing burnout and creating a positive work environment by:

- Using scheduling tools to balance workloads.
- Offering wellness programs and mental health support.
- Providing easy-to-use tools that simplify workflows.

Inspiration: Geisinger Health introduced digital tools to improve staff well-being, increasing job satisfaction by 25%.

7. Close the Gaps in Healthcare Access

Not everyone has equal access to care, but technology can help change that. Focus on:
- Expanding telemedicine to rural or underserved areas.
- Designing tools that are accessible to all, regardless of language or ability.
- Using data to understand and address health disparities.

Example: Partners In Health brought digital tools to remote communities, improving outcomes for patients who had been left behind.

A Success Story: Cleveland Clinic's Transformation

Cleveland Clinic's story shows how focusing on the Quintuple Aim can create real change:

- They used analytics to identify and help high-risk patients.
- Expanded telemedicine during the pandemic to make care more accessible.
- Automated admin tasks, saving costs and easing staff workloads.
- Extended virtual care to underserved areas, closing health equity gaps.

The results? Fewer hospital readmissions, happier patients, and a more efficient healthcare system.

Making It Last

To ensure your efforts are sustainable:

1. **Bring Everyone on Board**: Involve leadership, clinicians, and even patients in your planning.
2. **Embrace Change**: Provide training and support to help teams adapt.
3. **Measure and Adjust**: Use feedback and data to refine your strategy.
4. **Start Small**: Test solutions in one department before scaling up.

Chapter 14: Global Digital Transformation in Healthcare: Innovations Across Regions

The digital transformation of healthcare is reshaping how care is delivered worldwide. Through technologies like artificial intelligence (AI), telemedicine, blockchain, robotics, and IoT, healthcare systems are becoming more efficient, accessible, and patient-centered. This article consolidates global and regional insights, highlighting innovations and challenges in healthcare transformation.

North America

United States

The U.S. leads in leveraging cutting-edge technologies to enhance healthcare delivery:

AI in Diagnostics: Google Health developed AI systems that outperform radiologists in detecting breast cancer, reducing false negatives by 9% and false positives by 6%. Similarly, Mayo Clinic uses AI to analyze ECG readings, improving detection of cardiac conditions [52] [54].

Telemedicine Expansion: Teladoc Health facilitates remote chronic care management, helping reduce hospitalizations and improve patient outcomes. The U.S. Department of Veterans Affairs also uses telehealth services to reach veterans in rural areas [55] [56].

Canada

Canada's emphasis on **integrated EHR systems** has improved care continuity across its universal healthcare system. Telehealth initiatives have been particularly impactful in remote regions, expanding access for Indigenous communities [53].

Europe

Germany
The **ePA (Electronic Patient Record)** system allows patients to control and share their medical records securely, enhancing care coordination. During the pandemic, telemedicine platforms like **TeleClinic** gained popularity for virtual consultations and remote prescriptions 【62】 【66】.

France
AI tools like Therapixel improve breast cancer diagnostics, reducing errors in mammogram analysis. France also uses big data to predict hospital needs and optimize resource allocation during public health crises 【52】 【63】.

United Kingdom
The **NHS App** allows patients to book appointments, manage prescriptions, and access health records digitally. AI-powered platforms like Babylon Health's **GP at Hand** provide virtual consultations, reducing wait times for primary care 【62】 【64】.

Asia

China
China is at the forefront of healthcare digitization:
Smart Hospitals: Hospitals like Ping An Good Doctor integrate AI, IoT, and telemedicine for real-time diagnostics and patient monitoring 【52】 【65】.

During the COVID-19 pandemic, China employed big data to track outbreaks and allocate resources effectively 【65】.

Japan

Japan leads in robotics for elderly care, with robots like **PARO** and **Robear** assisting with mobility and providing mental health support. Precision medicine initiatives use AI to tailor cancer treatments, improving survival rates 【65】.

India
The **Ayushman Bharat Digital Mission** integrates health IDs and EHR systems across public and private sectors, improving access and streamlining patient management. Platforms like **Practo** and **eSanjeevani** have provided telehealth services to millions of rural patients 【66】.

AI tools such as Qure.ai analyze chest X-rays, aiding in early detection of diseases like tuberculosis 【54】 【66】.

Gulf Countries

Saudi Arabia
The **Seha App**, launched in 2018, conducted over 1.8 million virtual consultations by early 2020, improving access to care during the pandemic. Saudi Vision 2030 allocates $65 billion for healthcare transformation, focusing on AI, IoT, and blockchain for secure patient data management 【66】 【64】.

United Arab Emirates
Dubai Healthcare City leverages AI for predictive analytics and patient monitoring. Blockchain is being piloted for secure healthcare data sharing, enhancing interoperability across the UAE's healthcare ecosystem 【64】 【65】.

North Africa

Egypt
Telemedicine: Ain Shams University launched a virtual hospital to connect patients in rural areas with urban specialists, improving equitable healthcare access 【63】.

Egypt also uses big data to address non-communicable diseases and optimize public health interventions 【63】【64】.

Morocco
The Société Marocaine de Télémédecine (SMT) connects rural health centers to urban specialists, improving care for underserved populations 【63】.

Emerging Nations

Sub-Saharan Africa

Kenya: Platforms like mTiba enable mobile healthcare payments, increasing access for low-income families. AI tools also support TB and HIV diagnostics in rural areas 【62】【63】

South Africa: AI and IoT are being used for remote patient monitoring, particularly for chronic diseases like diabetes 【63】.

Latin America
Brazil and Argentina are expanding telemedicine to address physician shortages, especially in underserved regions 【63】.

Sources

- Neurosys: Digital Transformation in Healthcare 【52】
- Omnia Health Insights: Saudi Healthcare Transformation 【66】
- World Economic Forum: Digital Innovation in the Middle East 【62】
- Africa Health Exhibition: Big Data in African Healthcare 【63】
- Crunch Dubai: MENA Health Tech Landscape 【65】.

A Shared Mission for the Future of Care

As we come to the end of this journey together, I want to leave you with something more than just a plan or a strategy. I want to leave you with hope, hope for what healthcare can become and the role each of us can play in shaping its future.

Healthcare is deeply personal. It's about people and our loved ones, our communities, and ourselves. It's about ensuring that every person, no matter where they live or who they are, has access to care that is compassionate, timely, and life changing. For far too long, gaps in systems, data, and resources have stood in the way of this vision. But today, we have the power to change that.

The tools are already in our hands. The technologies we've discussed. AI, FHIR, telemedicine, and more are not just innovations; they're lifelines. They can prevent mistakes, save precious time, and make care accessible to those who have never had it before. But these tools mean nothing without the people who use them with care, purpose, and a shared commitment to making a difference.

This transformation is not just about technology or efficiency; it's about humanity. It's about restoring trust, dignity, and connection to a system that sometimes feels distant and overwhelming. It's about creating a future where patients feel seen, providers feel supported, and every person knows they matter.

This mission is bigger than any one of us. It requires courage to rethink what's possible, collaboration to break down barriers, and compassion to keep patients at the heart of every decision. But most importantly, it requires belief that we can do better and that the future of care is a future worth fighting for.

Together, we can build a future where healthcare is not a privilege, but a right. A future where every life is valued, and every patient receives the care they deserve. Let this be the start of something transformative not just for systems and technology, but for humanity.

Let's create that future together.

Diaa ElDin Helmy

Appendix A: Cross-Reference of the Quintuple Aim with Key Book Chapters

This appendix provides an easy-to-navigate guide for readers who want to dive deeper into the specific topics that align with the **Quintuple Aim** framework. Use the table below to find relevant chapters, sections, and tools that support each goal.

Quintuple Aim	Relevant Chapters & Sections	Key Tools & Concepts Covered
1. Improve Population Health	- **Chapter 4.1**: Data Analytics and Decision Support Systems - **Chapter 5.1**: Internet of Medical Things (IoMT)	- Predictive analytics for disease prevention. - Remote monitoring with wearables. - AI for chronic disease management.
	- **Chapter 7.1**: Precision Medicine and Genomics	- Data-driven insights to identify at-risk populations.
2. Enhance Patient Experience	- **Chapter 4.3**: Mobile Health (mHealth) and Wearable Devices	- Patient portals and apps for easy access. - Telemedicine for seamless virtual care.
	- **Chapter 3.4**: Benefits of Digital Transformation in Healthcare	- Real-time communication tools. - Improved transparency in care delivery.

Quintuple Aim	Relevant Chapters & Sections	Key Tools & Concepts Covered
3. Lower the Cost of Care	- **Chapter 3.5**: Challenges in Implementing Digital Transformation	- Automation of administrative processes to reduce waste. - ERP for supply chain optimization.
	- **Chapter 5.3**: Robotic Process Automation (RPA) and Robotics	- Cost-efficient resource allocation through AI.
4. Improve Staff Experience	- **Chapter 6.2**: Leadership and Change Management	- Building a supportive digital-first culture. - Overcoming resistance to change.
	- **Chapter 5.3**: Automation and Workflow Optimization	- Tools to reduce burnout by simplifying repetitive tasks.
5. Advance Health Equity	- **Chapter 4.3**: Telemedicine and Wearable Devices	- Expanding care to underserved populations through remote solutions.
	- **Chapter 7.1**: Precision Medicine and Genomics	- Personalized healthcare for marginalized groups.
	- **Chapter 5.1**: IoMT	- Addressing health gaps with connected devices.

Appendix B: Healthcare Digital Transformation Taxonomy

Term	Definition	Relevance to Digital Transformation
Population Health Management	The proactive management of a defined group's health outcomes through preventive care, monitoring, and data-driven interventions.	Supports the goal of improving population health using predictive analytics and IoT tools.
Patient Experience	The cumulative interactions and perceptions a patient has during their healthcare journey, encompassing convenience, communication, and care.	Enhances satisfaction and trust through digital tools like patient portals, telemedicine, and apps.
Predictive Analytics	The use of historical and real-time data to forecast patient outcomes and inform preventive measures.	Enables early detection of health risks and better resource allocation in care delivery.
Telemedicine	The remote delivery of healthcare services through video calls, apps, and other digital platforms.	Expands access to care, particularly for rural and underserved populations.

Term	Definition	Relevance to Digital Transformation
Internet of Medical Things (IoMT)	A network of connected medical devices and sensors that collect, analyze, and transmit patient health data in real time.	Facilitates remote monitoring and personalized care for chronic conditions.
Artificial Intelligence (AI)	The simulation of human intelligence in machines, enabling tasks like diagnosis, risk prediction, and administrative automation.	Improves decision-making, reduces costs, and enhances efficiency in healthcare workflows.
Robotic Process Automation (RPA)	The use of software robots to automate repetitive administrative tasks such as billing, claims processing, and scheduling.	Reduces operational costs and allows staff to focus on patient-centered activities.
Electronic Health Record (EHR)	A comprehensive, digital version of a patient's medical history, accessible across healthcare providers and systems.	Enhances interoperability and care coordination while reducing errors and inefficiencies.
Interoperability	The ability of different healthcare systems and technologies to exchange and interpret shared data seamlessly.	Ensures smooth data sharing, improving clinical decision-making and continuity of care.

Term	Definition	Relevance to Digital Transformation
Enterprise Resource Planning (ERP)	Integrated software systems that manage core hospital operations, including supply chain, HR, and financial processes.	Streamlines administrative functions and supports cost-efficiency in healthcare organizations.
Wearable Devices	Consumer-grade or medical-grade gadgets like fitness trackers or health monitors that collect data on users' physical and biological activity.	Provides real-time health insights for patients and clinicians, aiding in prevention and chronic disease management.
Change Management	The structured approach to transitioning individuals, teams, and organizations from their current state to a desired future state.	Essential for overcoming resistance and ensuring successful adoption of digital transformation initiatives.
Cybersecurity in Healthcare	The protection of sensitive health data and systems from cyber threats such as breaches, ransomware, and unauthorized access.	Ensures patient trust and compliance with regulations like HIPAA and GDPR.

Term	Definition	Relevance to Digital Transformation
Precision Medicine	A medical approach that tailors treatment to the individual characteristics of each patient, often based on genetic, environmental, or lifestyle data.	Leverages genomics and AI to provide highly targeted and effective care.
Blockchain in Healthcare	A decentralized ledger technology that ensures secure, transparent, and tamper-proof health data transactions.	Enhances data integrity, patient consent management, and traceability in the healthcare supply chain.
Big Data Analytics	The process of analyzing large volumes of complex healthcare data to uncover patterns and insights for better decision-making.	Drives innovations in population health, personalized medicine, and operational efficiency.
Virtual Reality (VR)	Immersive digital environments used for training, patient education, or therapeutic interventions.	Enhances medical education and patient outcomes, particularly in pain management and rehabilitation.
Augmented Reality (AR)	Technology that overlays digital information onto the real world, aiding diagnostics, education, or surgical planning.	Improves precision and patient understanding of medical procedures.

Term	Definition	Relevance to Digital Transformation
Genomics	The study of an organism's complete set of DNA, including gene interactions, to inform health interventions.	Enables breakthroughs in personalized treatments and predictive health strategies.
3D Printing in Healthcare	The creation of physical medical tools, prosthetics, or even biological tissues using 3D printing technologies.	Revolutionizes custom medical solutions, from prosthetics to organ bioprinting.
Data Privacy	The ethical and legal standards for managing and protecting patient data, ensuring confidentiality and compliance with regulations.	Builds trust and prevents misuse of sensitive health information.
Digital Twins	Virtual replicas of physical objects or systems, used to simulate and optimize healthcare processes or patient treatments.	Helps improve operational efficiency and predict patient outcomes in clinical trials or treatment planning.

Appendix C: List of Abbreviations

Abbreviation	Full Form
AI	Artificial Intelligence
ML	Machine Learning
NLP	Natural Language Processing
IoT	Internet of Things
IoMT	Internet of Medical Things
EHR	Electronic Health Record
EMR	Electronic Medical Record
HIS	Health Information System
ERP	Enterprise Resource Planning
RPA	Robotic Process Automation
API	Application Programming Interface
OCR	Optical Character Recognition
CDSS	Clinical Decision Support Systems
VR	Virtual Reality
AR	Augmented Reality
3D	Three-Dimensional
HIPAA	Health Insurance Portability and Accountability Act
GDPR	General Data Protection Regulation
DL	Deep Learning
GAN	Generative Adversarial Network
PCA	Principal Component Analysis
RNN	Recurrent Neural Network
K-NN	K-Nearest Neighbors
ASR	Automatic Speech Recognition
TTS	Text-to-Speech
LLM	Large Language Model
TOM	Target Operating Model

Abbreviation	Full Form
HL7	Health Level seven
FHIR	Fast Healthcare Interoperability Resources
IAAS	Infrastructure as a service
PAAS	Platform as a service
OCI	Oracle cloud infrastructure
KPI	Key Performance indicator
XML	Extensible Markup Language
BChain	Blockchain
DWH	Data Warehousing
SVM	Support Vector Machines
TKN	Tokenization
GAN	Generative Adversarial Network
CL	Clustering
K-M	K-Means Clustering
GPT	Generative Pre-trained Transformer
JSON	JavaScript Object Notation
FDA	Food and Drug Authority
B2B	Business to Business
B2C	Business to Customer
WHO	World Health Organization
NHS	National Health Service
ACA	Affordable Care Act
FAQs	Frequently Asked Questions
mHealth	Mobile Health
NGO	Non-Governmental Organization

www.ingramcontent.com/pod-product-compliance
Lightning Source LLC
Chambersburg PA
CBHW082250220526
45469CB00009B/2944